30 POEMS TO DANIELA

CAVENAGO

Published by
Picerni Publications
P.O. Box 12046
Dublin 2
Ireland

Print: Speciality Printing
Printed in Ireland

ISBN: 978-0-9568873-0-6

Picerni
Publications

I'd prefer if anyone reading these poems started reading them at the start and read through them as they were written in chronological order. It's a story.
Some of these poems can be seen on YouTube under "seán cavenago kavanagh"

TABLE OF CONTENTS

PREFACE

WAITING FOR THE SUN
(The 5th of September 1997)
(First poem I wrote to you Daniela for your birthday on the 3rd of July 1999)

All this time I've spent waiting,
My time consumed in health-centres, labour exchanges,
Doctors and dentists waiting rooms,
Thinking that this time was wasted
And nothing at all I could do about it.
Waiting at bus-stops, bar and shop counters
And in other various stalls,
Clocking up a life time of idle and endless queues.

When all along this time waiting was precisely fated
Into allowing me to be waiting in that exact place at that exact time,
Precisely weighted to coincide with you, although late,
To enter into the International bar punctually just after 2pm
On the 5th of September 1997
And sit down along that bar seat just up from mine.

Seán Caomhánach 22-June-1999 – 19/20P York Street

PROLOGUE – 30 POEMS TO DANIELA 30 POESIE A DANIELA

I said to you Daniela on the Monday the 10th of August 2009 at
Bonola Hospice Milano
And I was trying to work out a way to say it to you
A discreet way A delicate way
So I thought about it And I was thinking
'How am I going to phrase this to you'
I couldn't just come out And say to you "I'm going to write you 30 poems"
Or you'd of known I'd be writing them to you when you weren't here
anymore
So I said to you first "I'm thinking of taking up the poetry again"
And you said something like "Oh"
And then I said "Yea I'll write you 30 poems And you can read them"
And you said "Ah but we don't have any occasion It's not our
anniversary 'til September" (When we first met)
And I said
 "We've loads of occasions Daniela I'll write you 30 poems And you
can read them
Say "Si" Daniela"
You said "Si"
Eccoti.

Seán Caomhánach – Giovanni Cavenago – Seán Kavanagh

Poem 1 – *AMBULANCE BLUES*-AMBULANCE JOURNEY FROM VIA MAZZINI 28 ARLUNO TO BONOLA – 06-August-2009 – *ON THE BEACH*

That's two weeks ago now today Daniela
When the ambulance came to take you away And I was happy
To be going to hospital in an ambulance
Because I'd never been in an ambulance before
Because I thought they were going to fix the "Peristalsis" Fix you up
And get you eating again Build you up
So as you could get that experimental therapy in the IOE institute in Milan
And I was saying to you that we'd be out again in five days
And I was sort of disappointed
Because there was no siren sounding when we were in the ambulance
I'd of liked that
And that Neil Young song was humming in my head *Ambulance Blues*
But I couldn't think of what song it was at the time
And I was happy thinking you'd be out again in a few days
And I was saying that to you in the ambulance
Because I really believed it
But I should of known
But you told me it was a hospital we were going to
And when we got there after about seven hours
I realised it was a hospice because I knew the feel of hospitals by this stage
Knew it wasn't a hospital Knew it was a hospice
(Which you told me when I realised it was later that evening)
But I should of known it Copped it before
Because in that year and a half since the cancer was first diagnosed
As we left home in Via Mazzini 28
And you were lifted off the footpath from outside your gaff into the ambulance
That was the first time I had ever seen you crying
You weren't even crying
Just a few tears silently rolling down your big beautiful cheeks

And I wanted to lick them away as they strapped you into the
ambulance chair
Because now I know that you knew that you weren't coming home again
Except in that hearse six days later
When you were brought home again for your wake
And I'd never been in a hearse before either
And there was this terrible screeching siren sounding off inside of me.

Seán Caomhánach 20-August-2009 Via Mazzini 28 Arluno Milano Italia

Poem 2 – STELLA ALPINA – BONOLA – 12-AUGUST-09
– *DON'T WALK AWAY IN SILENCE*

Atmosphere
That last day
One of the doctors had told me just before out in the corridor
But I didn't understand everything but I did understand "Oggi" "Today"
But I was still thinking the evening or the night And at 11.30 that
last morning
I was watching that bone underneath your neck The breastbone I
think it's called
I was watching it slowly rising And then declining
And I was watching it for a while as it got slower
But then I just totally forgot about it Didn't bother looking at it anymore
And still holding your warm right hand in my warm left hand
Talking to you
Because I was never going to say good-bye to you
And I was talking And rubbing your arm
And telling you a few things we'd already said before
And anything that wasn't said before we already knew
So no need to be wasting precious breath
And about five minutes past 12 noon I whispered in your ear
"Vado per una sigaretta Torno subito"
And I kissed your cheek And I thought it a bit strange
Because your cheek was so cold
So I walked around the other side of the bed And kissed your other cheek
And that was so cold as well
But I passed no heed because your hand was warm
So I didn't realise it And when I came back a few minutes later
A nurse was there fiddling around with your catheter And looking
strangely at me-
Now I know the meaning of that expression on her face-
And I sat down again holding your warm right hand in my warm left hand
And rubbing your arm

And that nurse had gone out And come back with another nurse
And I still didn't realise it
Even with the two nurses on the other side of the bed
With those expressions on their faces And the nurse at the end of
your bed Cristina
Was calling me "Seán" to get my attention
And moving up towards the top of your bed
And indicating with her hands
And when she got to the top of your bed she felt your neck
And I think your face as well And whispered to me across your bed
"È morta Daniela è morta"
And I was still holding your warm right hand And I said
"Ma la mano è calda"
And I couldn't understand it because you must of been
Already dead for about half an hour
Those last few breaths slowly rising And then declining
And I was still there like a fuckin eejit not realising that
Even though you were dead
You had departed with your warm right hand in mine
And I had remained behind with my warm left hand in yours
Sempre.

21-August-2009 Arluno

Poem 3 – INTO AUGUST

Strange
After all the good times The laughs The rows The sex The drink
(Or me anyway)
All those things And all the bullshit that people think is important
It was towards the end when I saw your body being destroyed by
this disease
And as the doctor even said to me in the hospice about
Your heart And head staying strong
But your body was crumbling
And I remember helping you out to the bathroom
To wash your back at the beginning of August
And this flimsy gauze of see-thru skin draped over your boney bones now
And the big bloated thrombosis right foot totally out of proportion
With your scrawny skinniness And I remember your panic attacks at night
When you couldn't breathe And you said "Show me how to breathe Seán"
And the restless nights And wailing when you did get a bit of sleep
And the vomiting And the vomiting And the vomiting
Like you'd thrown up your insides out
And then the blood came up in the vomit basin And you said
"Is that blood Seán" And I'm looking in the basin at it And I said
"No Too light coloured"
What I didn't say to you was
'Too light coloured in comparison to the blood that was coming out
of your backside'
Or that green stuff the second last morning in the hospice
That was in the front of your knickers when I brought you out to the jacks
Well I don't know what the fuck that was
But I even made a joke about how you must of drank too much
Of that "Granita" mint drink you used to throw up
Because when I saw you so weak And how this disease did destroy
dismantle you
Where sometimes you were barely able to whisper

Where I had to lift you on And off the toilet seat "Uno due tre su"
Knowing how dignified And independent you are But
Strange
After all the good times The laughs The rows The sex The drink
(Or me anyway)
All those things And all the bullshit that people think is important
When I saw you like this
I knew the importance of what you had taught me
For when I saw you like this
I knew for sure then what it was like to feel love.

22-August-2009 Arluno

Poem 4 – I BEI GIORNI ANDATI

I remember
It must of been about seven years ago
After one of them rows that we had
Could never remember what they were about afterwards
Except that they were always about nothing
And then there was the usual week of silence
I was real good at silence
And there'd be no eye contact either
And I was out walking about a week later And not looking ahead
And just there at the junction of Stephen And Longford Streets Uppers
Where the streets widen across each other
And I ran straight into you
My eyes didn't have a chance to avoid your *Pair Of Brown Eyes*
And your smile stretched from one footpath over as far as the other
And what else could I do but fall into them
And then I remember about three years before that again
Another row another week of fuming silence
And I was walking up York Street near the corner with "The Green"
With a grumpy head on me
It was an Easter Saturday because I remember thinking
'Yea you'd be getting your Easter egg the next day alright
Waiting on the table for you in the morning smashed up in little pieces'
And I was walking up York Street near the corner with "The Green"
With a grumpy head on me
And I ran straight into you again coming the other way
(You must of been coming home from your shift in the Conrad in
Earlsfort Terrace)
And before I knew it I was looking at you
And you were looking at me
And you were smiling at me
And I was smiling at you
And then you were laughing

And then I was laughing
And then we were both laughing together
And then we took each others hands
Said nothing to each other
But just laughed And laughed all the way to Easter Sunday.

23-August-2009 Arluno

Poem 5

I miss the rows Daniela
The passion The melodrama Always spectacular
And always about upping the ante And who could land
The lowest dirtiest blow
And I remember that stand up row we had
In the old York Street about ten years ago
And we were squaring up to each other
And you were pointing your finger at me And roaring
"I'm tougher than you I'm tougher than you"
And I'm roaring back going
"Yea yeah yeahh Sure you are Sure you are"
And I felt like breaking your fuckin Italian neck
And for some reason
I remembered this row when we were in Bonola hospice
When I seen your courage And your spirit
'Yea yeah yeahh Sure you are Sure you are
Way tougher than me'
And you were complaining a few months before this around last March
"I've lost my anger This disease has taken away my anger"
But from where I was watching And listening
You said it with perfect anger so I said nothing
Or on that last Sunday the 9th of August in the hospice
Three days before you died when you sat up in the bed
With your left fist clenched proclaiming
"Viva la Vita Viva la Vita"
And laughing And hooping "Uh huh Uh huh"
Or on that last Monday two days before you died
When I was sitting on your bed And you eye-balled me And you said
"I love you tanto And I won't give up"
And I was thinking to meself
'Give up Daniela give up You can't win this'
But I knew your strength of character to want to take it on

And I drew strength from you And I said to meself
"I'm not giving up either"
For those terrible days when I used to thank God
For another day with you But
I miss the rows Daniela
The passion The melodrama Always spectacular
Because it's not the same
Because now I've just gone back
To rowing with meself again.

27-August-2009 Dublin

Poem 6 – I KNOW YOU WILL

I don't want to go into this Daniela
So you have to help me
It's your turn now
Because I don't want to go into this
So help me.

29-August-2009 Sráid Eabhrac BAC 2

Poem 7 – PICERNI PASQUALE (MARIANNO PICERNO)

I sit And talk
Or more so listen to your father now a lot but I always did
Always loved him even if he's there
A 90 year old man with dementia And one arm
And they say he doesn't know anything about his only child passing
But I know he senses something
And we're on the armchairs turning around to each other
And he's talking to me
Because he likes talking to me And I like listening to him
Even if it's difficult for me to always understand what he's saying
Because his 90 year old dementia voice is a bit weak
And then sometimes I think he's throwing in bits of his Arlunese dialect
And then sometimes I think he's throwing in bits of his original
Basilicata dialect
But he's the exact same eyes as you
And the same skin And the same face And the same habits And the
same tastes
And the same "Bersaglieri" head
Because there's a man who never had to worry about
Not being the father of his daughter
So I'm looking at him And saying "Si Pasquale Si Pasquale"
Or "Papy" as I call him now
And I laugh when he laughs
And I look sad when he looks sad And nod my head profoundly
Even if I know that he's probably talking again about the war
Or his birthplace down south in Tito
Or where he worked in Milan fifty years ago
Or his brother Antonio who's been dead for years
And he doesn't even know it
But I know he likes talking to me
And I like listening to him
Even if it's difficult for me to always understand what he's saying

So I'm looking at him And saying "Si Papy Si Papy"
And I laugh when he laughs
And I look sad when he looks sad And nod my head profoundly
Just so
As I can look straight into his eyes
And see your eyes looking back at me.

3-September-2009 Arluno

Poem 8 – CHE CAZZO È SUCCESSO DANIELA

I was always sure of you Daniela
Nearly right from the start on the first day you arrived over to me
And me bell rang on the 8th of September 1997
And I looked out me window from the fourth floor And you were
Down on the street at the front hall-door
Looking up at me waving And smiling
And you brought me two cans of Heineken And a can of Becks
And a coffee-cake you'd bought in Superquinn in Sutton
And I thought 'This is grand' because by that time
I'd already drank me last two or three cans that were in the fridge
So I was always sure of you
And after about two weeks together
And we were lying in the bed
And you said "I want to tell you something"
And I said "Go ahead and tell me so And don't be making a big
Italian opera out of everything"
And you said "No you'll only laugh"
And I said "No I won't laugh"
And then you said "I love you"
And I started laughing
But it was just nervous laughter
Because a woman had never said that to me before
Because I was always sure of you nearly right from the start
Like that time you arrived over to me Maybe after about two
months together
And you had a few days off from Caffè Caira in Howth
And you were coming over to spend them with me
And you rang the bell And came up
And I'd left the hall door open for you
And I'd went to the corner boiling the electric kettle on the fridge
And I was there making me tea Making me wary distance
When I heard this banging thud on the floor

And I turned around with me cup of tea in me hand
And you'd dropped your luggage bag with such force on the floor
And you were charging across it at me And I said
"Mind me tea" And I managed to get it onto the fridge in time
And you charged *Into My Arms* to overwhelm me
Or a while later I came home drunk one evening
And made straight for the bed but didn't make it as far as the bed
But fell asleep on me way on the bedroom floor I was that drunk
And I was awoken by these kicks into me chest And stomach
And I sobered up quick enough
And I was fuckin bullin And going on about domestic violence
And the "Emergency battered bloke line"
And I can get drunk anytime I want without getting kicked when I'm
sleeping on the floor "And you knew what I was like when you first
met me you fuckin cunt And if you don't like it there's the door get out"
But you wanted to be my saviour
Your water-sign for my destruction of fire Glendalough (Ricordi)
And I'm roaring at you "Get the fuck out"
And you started mouthing off "No I won't go"
And I got you in a headlock And dragged you to the door roaring
"Get out get the fuck out" And your roaring
"No no I won't go I won't go"
And I got you as far as the door after a struggle
Had a real good grip on you
But I had to release my right hand a bit
So as to release the latch on the door
And you wriggled a bit out of the headlock
But I got a hold of you again
And I'm trying to kick the door open with my left foot
And you're trying to kick the door closed with your left foot
And I'm roaring "Get the fuck out"
And your roaring "No I won't go"
And we're tussling And struggling
And I nearly had you over the threshold a few times Over the line

But you kept wriggling lose And retreating back into the hallway
again roaring
"No I won't go I won't go"
And after about ten or fifteen minutes of this I was just bollixed tired
So I just stopped
Because I knew I couldn't put you out so I just left it thinking to meself
'I won't be trying this again'
And went in And sat down on me armchair
Trying to get me breath back
And I'm not happy
And I'm not sad
Because this day has opened my eyes
But I'm angry with you
But I'm happy with you
Because I could still hear your shouting resounding in my ears
"I won't go I won't go"
I knew you meant it
Because I knew you were insecure about us at the start
But you didn't know that I was even more insecure about us than you
Because I hid it
Buried it way down deep inside of me
Where no one could ever touch it or use it against me
And I was happy as I got my breath back
Because I was sure of you And still hearing "I won't go I won't go"
And I think I spent the first year or so doing me best to drive you
away from me
Probably just so as I could say to meself after "I was fuckin right"
And I used to love the way you'd mispronounce words
When you'd say to me after that
"You try to put me at the door"
Nothing about kicking me in the chest And stomach
When I was sleeping on the bedroom floor though Oh no Only
"You try to put me at the door"
Worse than me for repeating yourself

At least I'd usually have the excuse of been drunk for the most of mine
"You try to put me at the door"
I thought I'd never hear the end of it until eventually one day I had to
say it to you
"No Daniela Not **at** the door I had you **at** the door   That was the
easy bit It was **out** the door I was trying to put you"
(Or when you'd call over And you'd stop at Bewley's for a coffee
And steal the sugar sachets for me And I'd say
"Ah my great thief All you do for me")
And I was thinking this morning that tomorrow will be
Our twelfth anniversary of the day we first met
And we had twelve great years together
Where I was always sure of you
(And I used to say to you "You're only after me for me dole money Daniela"
And you'd laugh And say "Yea Seán I'm only after you for your dole
money")
But I don't know what's happening now
But I remember the 8th of June this year
It's not even three months ago in St Vincent's hospital
And I never told you the full story about that day Daniela
When I came out from seeing the liaison nurse
And you were sitting on a wheelchair in the corridor of St. Anne's Ward
And you said "Are you crying" And I said "No"
And I wasn't either but I couldn't face you
After what I'd just been told And I was heading for the waiting room
Just to get away from you for a while And compose meself a bit
And you called me "Seán" And I turned around to you And you said
"I won't leave you"
And that's not even three months ago
And I'm supposed to feel lucky
That I had those twelve great years with you but I don't
Because I got up this morning
And I went into the bathroom
And I was at the wash-basin sink

Washing the water into me eyes And washing the water out of me eyes
When I caught a glimpse of meself in the mirror
And I just stopped And stared at you
And asked the same question
Always the same question
"What the fuck happened Daniela
What the fuck happened"

4-September-2009 Arluno

Poem 9 – ONION

You'd sent me out for an onion that morning
You must of been planning on cooking risotto that evening
And it was early enough Must of been a Saturday
As there was hardly any traffic or people around
And I was glad to get out
Needed to walk And have time on my own to think
Because you were really up my arse about my past
My history with women And I didn't know what to tell you
And I was feeling the pressure The constant questions
Because as far as I was concerned
All's that mattered was from the 5th of September 1997
And everything before that date was irrelevant
And I hated being asked questions anyway Except in a quiz
Like in that first year or two when you'd ask me
Where I was going And I hated being asked that question so I said
"Oh Venezuela or maybe the Bahamas or maybe the Seychelles"
And after a while you'd cracked my code to realise that
Venezuela was the International bar
The Bahamas was Grogan's bar And
The Seychelles was the Swan bar
And you always knew where to find me
But that morning of the onion
I could feel you closing in on me
And I didn't know how to react
And I said to you once
"Just because you're a woman you think you're the only one who's
touchy around here meet me meet me And I'll fuckin show you what
touchy is"
And I'd tried putting you at the door a few times
Because you were getting too close
But then you'd start crying
And I'd fall for it because I sort of knew that

You were genuine in your explosions of emotion And I said
"Stop crying will you you fucking sap you can stay"
And you'd stop crying And then you'd be laughing
With the tears coming down your cheeks
And I'd lick them all away And you said
"I am a fuckin sap Your sap"
But that morning I was feeling under pressure
And I didn't know what to do
Apart from buying the onion in the greengrocers on Wexford Street
And after buying it I kept on walking up Camden Place And
Onto Heytesbury Street And I was thinking
'I can't tell you I can't trust you'
And you were really up my arse about my past
My history with women And I didn't have one
And me And me onion were walking down Grantham Street
And I was thinking 'You want to know too much about me'
And I didn't want anybody knowing anything personal about me
And I was thinking I'm going to have to get out of this I have to
You're asking too many questions
I want my peace back And I was thinking
'You're a woman doing your intelligence-gathering on me
Digging for my weakness Scraping for my vulnerability
Just so as you can use it against me
Throw it back in my face the first chance you get then'
And I don't know what I'd of done if you'd of done that so
Fucked if I was going to gift you with any ammunition
And me And me onion were walking down Camden Street
Because I'd already a real low opinion of meself And full of self-hatred
Believed I was repulsive
The enemy within the camp
The enemy within meself
And that's the only enemy that's ever got to be overcome
But that morning my head was bursting with the pressure
And I even thought of inventing a few women for you

But I wasn't going to lie to you
And it wasn't at this time

(It was after this time I fast forward
You were always trying to boost me Build up my confidence
And always saying to me "You're beautiful Seán You're beautiful"
And I said "You're full of shit"
And you said "But you are beautiful Seán"
And I said "Would you ever go And fuck off with yourself And leave
me alone"
And you kept saying this to me Right up into my face for over ten years
And you'd be singing this song to me
You are so beautiful my winter love
I'd just ignore you but now I think you just made up that song yourself
Because you kept saying it to me trying to boost me
"You're beautiful Seán" until I think you really believed it
And I said "Fuck off with yourself I'm trying to watch the telly"
And you said "But you are You're beautiful"
And I said "And you're fuckin nuts"
And you said "But you're beautiful Seán You are"
And I said "Would you ever leave me alone you fuckin nutcase"
And you said "You're beautiful Seán"
And I said "I am in my bollocks"
And you said "Say it Seán say it say you're beautiful"
And I said "No Because it's not true"
But I wasn't going to lie to you
Because my logic is
That if I lie to you it means that I'm afraid of you
And I was never going to be afraid of you
Although at the end your courage did frighten me a bit
But you kept at it relentlessly
"Say it Seán say it say your beautiful"
"No I won't fuckin say it because it's not true"
"Say it Say it Say it Say you're beautiful Seán"

And one day I said to you when you were at it again
"Ok Daniela Maybe in your eyes I'm beautiful but you're not objective"
And then you said
"Ok Seán In my eyes you're beautiful So say what you are in my eyes
Say it say it
In my eyes what are you Say it Seán Say it"
Oh very clever very clever My clever little Italian woman
You walked me right into that one
And I hated being outsmarted by you Which was rare
Because after a while I'd sort of conceded that you might
Possibly be tougher than me alright Just might
But I'd comforted meself with thinking
That I was smarter than you
And that's more important)

(Or them other times when we'd be playing
Them marathon "La scala" card games not for money
But for pride And passion
Especially when we'd be up the mountain at Sueglio
And you always managed to win the card games overall
By just one game
I've been thinking about that
How did you do that
Always managing to win the card games overall
By just one game
When we'd be playing "La scala"
And you'd still have all thirteen cards in your hands
And I might just have the one left
And I'd be thinking 'Yes I have you now This time Victory'
And then you'd put down all your thirteen cards in one go
You'd be out Game over
And you'd lean across the table laughing And say to me
"That's class"
' That hurt'

And I'd always try to spoil your victory
"Ah you were fuckin cheatin" A bad loser
But if it was anyone else in this world who I'd lost a game of cards to
I wouldn't of given it a fuckin damn
But with you Daniela it was personal
I suppose I can tell you now Daniela
I hated losing those "La scala" card games to you And you saying
"That's class"
And I tried your trick a few times
Just to get out with all thirteen cards in one go like you could
To lay all my thirteen cards down in one go on the table
I'd be out Game over
And lean across the table laughing And say to you
"That's class"
But I could never do it)

"So say it Seán In my eyes what are you Say it"
"In your eyes I'm beautiful but you're not objective"
And me And me onion as we were walking down Wexford Street again
We didn't know any of this back then
And onto Kevin Street And around again to Camden Street And
Wexford Street again
And onto Cuffe Street And Mercer Street And I was thinking
'No I can't trust you I don't have to you can fuck off with yourself
And your questions
I'll put you at the door I have to get out of this you're getting too close'
And me And me onion were on "The Green"
And I decided to go home thinking
I'd put you at the door
Or not knowing what I was thinking
And walking up York Street I was getting closer to you
And I got to the door I decided
I'm going to have to take a risk with you
I'm going to have to tell you

I'm going to have to trust you
And me And me onion got in the door
And you were still in bed And I said to you
"About this past This history of mine with women
I don't have one You're it You're my history"
And maybe you were relieved that it wasn't personal And you said
"I thought something all right but I thought you'd been raped or
something like that
I thought you hated me"
And I said "No Nothing like that I'm just not used to being touched
Not used to it
It makes me nervous Simple as that"
And then I sort of threatened you
"I don't ever want to hear this mentioned again ok"
And you never mentioned it again
And you never used it against me
And you never threw it back in my face
And I will always be grateful to an onion.

7-September-2009 Arluno

Poem 10

I look at that photograph now of you Daniela
And I see your right cheek so clear
And I think how many times did I kiss
And lick that cheek
And I'd lick away the tears after a row
And you'd start laughing
And then there'd be even more tears
In your laughter
And I'd lick them all away
Give me your tears Daniela
And I'll lick them all away
And I'd lick your eyes
And I'd lick your nose
And I'd lick your lips
And I'd lick your tongue
Lick away my tears now Daniela.

15-September-2009 York Street

Poem 11 – CABBAGE

I'm thinking fondly nostalgically
About some of them great rows we used to have Daniela
Can't remember what the most of them were about
But there's two that particularly stand out in my memory
Because they were that ridiculous
And the one about the cabbage has to be
The greatest farce of a row in the history of the human race
About five years ago Don't know how it started
But I do know that it was you that started it as usual
And you started mouthing off about
How the Savoy cabbage was the best cabbage in the world
And I copped it that you were only saying this
Because the Savoy cabbage is the Italian cabbage
Called after the old royal family that reigned in Italy
So I reacted straight away
"No the Irish cabbage is far superior And tastier compared to that
Savoy Italian rubbish that you wouldn't even feed to pigs"
And I knew that you only ate cabbage about maybe once a year
When you'd eat "La casöra" in Italy
And I only ate cabbage about maybe once a year also
And I knew that you or me didn't give a shite about cabbage
But this developed into a cultural nationalistic inter-nationalistic row
Which escalated into a patriotic one
About which country had the best quality cabbage
And this became the principle
And before I knew it the two of us
Were after getting really worked up about cabbage
And roaring And shouting at each other And I said
"Ah Savoy cabbage And that Savoy family who would feed their
cabbage to their pigs before they'd give it to the people who were
starving such was their "respect" for the people   Thought more of

their pigs than the people the dirty royalist imperialist running-dog
bastards And there's you praising And promoting their cabbage-
Some communist you are Some communist you are".
Oh you didn't like that
And I was delighted with meself
And I think we didn't speak to each other for only a couple of days
after that one
As it was such a clear cut victory for me
And I was in too good a humour after it
So I could afford to be gloatingly generous
And not my usual vindictive self
Because I knew I'd really sickened you with me argument
And I was thinking afterwards
That if you had of used your head
You could of got me back real easy
But I wasn't going to gift you with any ammunition against me
So I said nothing about the "Irish" cabbage Daniela because
That's actually "York" cabbage
So you could of hit back And said to me
"Oh "Irish" cabbage "York'" cabbage you mean That crowd who
would feed their cabbage to their pigs before they'd give it to the
people who were starving such was their "respect" for the people
Thought more of their pigs than the people the dirty royalist
imperialist running-dog bastards And there's you praising And
promoting their cabbage-
Some republican you are Some republican you are".

18-September-2009 Arluno

Poem 12 – MAMMA MIA

I was watching the telly on me armchair
Maybe about five years ago
Watching it but not interested in it
And it was the *Sopranos* that was on
But I'd never followed it or got into it
When you started going on about it And you said
"They are not Italians We don't speak like that"
And I said "No they're not Italians They're Italian-Americans"
And then you said
"No they are not Italians They're Sicilians"
And I'm starting to get pissed-off with you And I'm counter-attacking
"Yea And Sicily is in Italy so that makes them 100 percent Italian"
And it's starting to escalate again over nothing
And I knew your form I'd done my own little bit of intelligence-
gathering on you
So I knew the way you'd hover around me armchair
Trying to block me view of the telly
Trying to spoil me enjoyment of it
And I wasn't even enjoying it
But I started to enjoy it just out of spite
Because I wasn't having you dictating to me
What I watch on my telly "You fuckin Mussolini you"
And then some character in the *Sopranos* said
"Mamma Mia"
And you went berserk And came out with another one of your
infallible proclamations
"Nobody in Italy says Mamma Mia never ever"
And at this stage I'm starting to get really wound up And I said
"Yes everybody in Italy says Mamma Mia always everyday every
second they say it
I know I've been there And they never stop saying it"
And you said

"No we never ever say Mamma Mia"
And I said "Yea" and you said "No"
"Yea no yea no yea no yea no yea no" "Yea"
Because after about two years of rowing with you I just got into the mantra
Because before that I'd be making rational points And logically
constructed arguments
But after about two years of rowing with you I realised it was wasted
on you
And why should I invest my intelligence in constructing arguments
When they weren't being appreciated
"No we're not arguing about that We're arguing about this"
So I just got into the mantra
Because I'd no choice
Because you'd be there responding to my carefully constructed
arguments
With a load of old irrelevant shite
And mouthing off about stuff that had nothing got to do
With the argument that we were supposed to be having
And I wasn't going to be distracted by your diversionary tactics
So I got into the mantra
A short snappy slogan of about four or five words
And just keep repeating this
And why should I be getting worked up about an argument
When you weren't even listening to it And then you'd say
"You don't listen to me"
"No you don't listen to me"
"No you don't listen to me"
"No you don't listen to me"
Paganini non ripete
And we'd a ferocious row about this that went on
Long after that episode of the *Sopranos* had finished
I never got to see that episode at all because of you
And I never watched it again
Because I never followed it in the first place anyway Never got into it

And you were still going berserk about stereotypes
Although you weren't saying anything
About that *Simpson's*-snake episode that stereotyped the Irish Oh no
And you were sitting on your couch laughing
And I'm sitting on me armchair definitely not laughing
I didn't laugh once And I'm sniping at you
"What are you laughing at That's not funny How is that funny"
Spoiling your enjoyment Getting me own back
Even if I did think it was funny
I wasn't telling you that
And I remember a few weeks after that "Mamma Mia" row
Which afterwards we didn't speak to each other for a week over that one
And we were in Italy on holidays that summer
Sitting outside Petit bar under the sun in Arluno
With a few of your Italian friends
And what did I hear coming out of your mouth only
"Mamma Mia" And slapping your hands on your knees
And you didn't just say it the once
And I was righteously glaring across the table at you
Trying to get your attention
Oh you knew I was righteously glaring across the table at you
Trying to get your attention
With your "Mamma Mia" you fuckin hypocrite you
And there's us just after having a row about it that went on for a week
And now your coming out with your "Mamma Mia"
With a few of your Italian friends And having a laugh
And I was trying to get your attention
Because I was just going to lip whisper at you across the table
Discreetly between you And me I was just going to lip whisper
"Mamma Mia"
And I was thinking 'I'm going to remember this'
'I'll store this little treasure away for use at a future date'
'You And your "Mamma Mia" are getting this back'
And you knew I was righteously glaring across the table at you

But you wouldn't look over at me
Too busy laughing And saying "Mamma Mia"
Thought you'd deprive me of my victory
No no chance the next row you're going to hear all about "Mamma Mia"
I have the evidence
But we were on holidays
Sitting outside Petit bar under the sun in Arluno
Having a few beers And a few laughs
And I just let it go
Never did use that treasure of ammunition
Never mentioned it to you again
Never watched the *Sopranos* again either
And when I'm in Italy And I hear someone saying "Mamma Mia"
As they always everyday do
I can never stop smiling about that row that went on for a week with you.

21-September-2009 Arluno

Poem 13 – UNO DUE TRE SU – *INTO MY ARMS*

I remember our routine when I'd lift you up
I'd put my arms under your shoulders
And I'd say "Uno due tre su"
And I'd lift you up
And you'd snuggle your face into my shoulder
And burrow your head across my chest
And we'd stay like that for a while
Singing that Nick Cave song *Into My Arms*
Except I kept singing the words wrong to you "Into your arms"
There ain't nobody that can sing like me
And them moments were our peace And happiness then
And just there this morning your father was at the table
Struggling to get up from it
"Lazarus" you used to call him
Because he could be there for an hour trying to stand up
And never wants any help His daughter's father
But he always manages to eventually
Stand up on his own two feet independently
But just this morning I could see him struggling
To get up off his chair at the table
And I was wary about asking him if he wanted help
Because he's always polite And courteous
Except when you ask him if he wants help he takes it as an insult
And I was wary that he might insult me back
But I asked him if he wanted a help up
And I was surprised when he said "Si"
Not like "Lazarus" to say that
So I took his right hand firmly in mine And I said to him
"Uno due tre su" And up got "Lazarus" with a "Grazie"
And that's my moment of peace And happiness for today Daniela.

22-September-2009 Arluno

Poem 14 – SNAILS

Meself and Nina were just up at the cemetery
There this morning Daniela
And there was two snails on the side of your grave stuck to each other
And Nina didn't like to see the snails on the side of your grave
And she asked me to throw them so I did
But if it was left to me I'd of left them there
For they were stuck so closely to each other
And seemed so safe And snuggled up inside their shells together
And I picked them up And put them into the palm of me left hand
As I walked over to that green cemetery bin
I was looking at them to see
Trying to figure out who
Which of them was you
And which of them was me.

23-September-2009 Arluno

Poem 15 – IL TUO GIARDINO DANIELA

There was a bit of a commotion
When I got to your parents gaff last Monday evening Daniela
Your father was standing at the table
Wanting to go to the cemetery
I thought at first that it must of meant that he wanted to die
But he's his daughter's father
And he won't give up either
And they say he doesn't know anything about his only child passing
But I know he senses something
Because he wanted to go And visit the cemetery
Because he's hearing all the talk about the cemetery in the gaff
And taking in bits of it even if he has dementia
So I suggested we don't refer to "Il cimitero" anymore
But in future we call it "Il giardino"-"The garden"
But I didn't say anything about the double significance of this word
But you know Daniela what I mean when I talk about your garden
Because I was your gardener
And I took real good care of your garden
The only work I ever loved "Il bel lavoro"
And I tended it with devoted husbandry
And nurtured all its natural beauty cultivating
Garofani Rossi Gigli Rossi Rose Rosa Fucsie Felici Fantasie di Fiori
I grew all those flowers with my green-fingered
Touch like a sun-tongue opening petal lips
With still the morning dew moist on them like a good night kiss
Where it was always an Italian summer
And the withering of winter never fell
And you used to say I was the best gardener in the world
But sure that was easy when you'd the most beautiful garden in the world
But sure that was easy because I loved your garden
Always loved entering my garden.

24-September-2009 Arluno

Poem 16

I remember once we were talking Daniela
Can't remember exactly when
A few years ago
And we were talking about
How lucky we were to have met each other
And you said
"If I didn't meet you I would only be an old spinster living alone in Milan"
And I said
"Sure if I didn't meet you I'd already be a dead drunkard in Dublin"
And I remember your laugh A strange laugh
Never heard any laugh remotely like it before
And when I'm alone And it's silent
I always try to hear your laugh
Because I don't find it getting any easier with time
It just sinks in more Deeper And deeper
So I always try to hear your laugh rising And arising.

24-September-2009 Arluno

Poem 17 – GOOD QUALITY

That used to really annoy me Daniela
When I'd get up in the morning or the afternoon
And all me clothes would be missing
And replaced by newly washed pressed And ironed ones
And that used to drive me nuts when you'd do that
A violation And contravention of my human rights
Under international law
Because it takes me a few days to feel comfortable in me clothes
And after a few months I'm really feeling comfortable in them
And I'd get up all angry then saying
"Where's all me fuckin clothes disappeared to"
And I'd raid the washing basket
And take them all out again
And model proudly around the gaff in them
"It's a man's right to be scruffy if he wants That's my right"
And you were trying to turn me into some
Ben vestito ben curato well dressed elegant fashionable Milan man
Well that's not my culture Me ne frego Ne ho diritto
Because my rights And culture is scruffy
And I'd even hide me clothes at night
But the gaff was too small Too easy to find
And then you started putting them into the washing machine
Before I'd get up out of the bed
So as to avoid leaving me clothes in the washing basket
So I'd have to put on the newly washed pressed And ironed ones
But I'd still make me protest by getting them
And crumpling And creasing them all up again and saying
"Ah that's better Now I feel more comfortable"
Because it used to piss me off when you'd steal me clothes
A sneak attack when I was sleeping And I know my rights
My right to be scruffy Ne ho diritto Not my culture
The ben vestito ben curato well dressed elegant fashionable Milan man

And you'd waste the weekend ironing with your Italian iron
On your Italian ironing board
And I'd be sitting there invisibly on the margins of me armchair
Disempowered dependent And emasculated
Feeling very vulnerable
Drinking me cup of tea or a can of beer at the weekends watching the telly
Going on about the tyranny I was living under
And going on about Mussolini
Where I couldn't even dress the way I wanted
Or wear the clothes the way I wanted
And about how my culture And heritage was being destroyed
As the most oppressed species on the planet The Irish man
"You fuckin Mussolini you" You didn't like that
But I should of called you "Berlusconi" instead
Because you'd of liked that even less
But I just never thought of it
Or when we were in the hardware shop on Wexford Street there last April
And you seen the Framar step-ladder And you said
"It's an Italian step-ladder Good quality"
And I said "But we don't need a step-ladder"
And you said "But it's an Italian step-ladder Good quality Good quality"
And I said "But we don't need a step-ladder"
And you said "But it's an Italian step-ladder Good quality Good quality"
And I said " But we don't need a step-ladder And besides an Irish
step-ladder would be far better quality but if you want to waste thirty
euro on your Italian step-ladder go ahead I'm tall you're small"
And after carrying your Italian step ladder back to the new gaff
You weren't getting away with it so I said about Fiat
"A heap of shit A shit Italian car Shit quality Shit quality" And you said
"Ah that's because it's all robots assembling the cars there now
And the few workers that are working there They are not Italians"
And I'm last wording it "But it's still an Italian car"
And I don't know what that discussion was about Daniela
Because neither of us could drive

Neither of us had ever driven a car in our lives
Italian or any other nationality
But you weren't getting away with it
And then blowing on about how everything Italian was better than Irish
And then there's your Italian washing machine Zanussi "Good
quality Good quality"
Well that Italian washing machine won't be so dizzy
From all the spinning it used to get
When I do eventually learn how to turn it on
Or your Zanussi Italian cooker "Good quality Good quality"
Well that Italian cooker won't be getting used so much either
But maybe as a compromise I'll be frequenting more regularly
An Italian fish 'n' chip shop instead
"We don't eat fish 'n' chips in Italy Nobody eats fish 'n' chips in Italy
only the idiot Irish drinking cappuccino in the afternoons And
evenings thinking they're trendy
Nobody in Italy drinks cappuccino after eleven in the morning"
And every other Italian thing in the gaff in Dublin
Won't be getting used so much
Because going into the gaff in Dublino
Is like going into "Little Italy"
And when I got back to Dublin in September after your death
Well that Italian step-ladder that you got
The "Good quality Good quality" Framar one because it's Italian
And it's out on the balcony
But it won't close so yea Daniela you were definitely right again as usual
Doesn't close properly so it's definitely an Italian step-ladder alright
And a good quality Irish beer crate
Would of served the purpose for standing up on far more effectively
"An Irish beer crate Good quality Good quality"
But wait 'til I get back to our Italian gaff in Dublino again
And you'll see the real me
And I'll say to you like what you used to say

About what your cousin used to say sarcastically about people from Veneto
But I say it with sincerity
"You're 100 percent Italian Daniela"
MADE IN ITALY
Good quality Good quality My Daniela.

25-September-2009 Arluno

Poem 18 – 1st OF JUNE 2009 – PERE LACHAISE CEMETERY – PARIS

We were sitting on the side of the footpath
Under the cover of those tall trees
That reach out over the wall from Pere Lachaise cemetery Paris
After doing our walking tour of it
And you were smoking And resting
While we were talking about Jim Morrison And Oscar Wilde
And you used always go there on pilgrimage for Jim Morrison's
anniversary
The 3rd of July (Like Brian Jones also you'd say too)
Because that day was your birthday
And we'd been talking about going there for years
So we're sitting on the side of the footpath
Outside Pere Lachaise cemetery Paris
Talking about Jim Morrison And Oscar Wilde
And you were delighted that you had the strength
To walk right around that huge cemetery And out again
And it was the first day of June
And we'd said we'd go to Paris for four days for our fourth wedding
anniversary
And as we were talking on the footpath outside the cemetery
I noticed a brown crinkled withered winter leaf
Fall on your back And cling to it
Must of fallen from one of those tall trees
That reach out over the wall at Pere Lachaise cemetery
And I was trying to look around behind us discreetly
Without you knowing what I was looking around for
And I scanned And scrutinised all them trees
Looking for one that grew brown crinkled withered winter leaves
But I couldn't see any
Except for that one that was still clinging to the back of your jacket
And I was wondering 'Where did that come from'
For maybe it came from Jim Morrison or Oscar Wilde

Who had reached out over the wall at Pere Lachaise cemetery
Under the cover of those tall tress
And pinned that brown crinkled withered winter leaf onto your back
As if to claim you
And it was from then I think my superstition began to foresee
That winter would fall on you prematurely.

29-September-2009 Arluno

Poem 19 – I TAKE MY SMALL BLESSINGS

I take my small blessings
Anytime we left the gaff for going away
Milano Paris Strokestown Turloughmore Belfast Free Derry
Expensive Kerry
Ireland 32 And 33 Liverpool
Just inside the hall door Drop our luggage on the floor
Throw our arms around each other
And swap a big wet kiss
And I was wondering And dreading
How the fuck was I going to do this
When the time came to go to the hospice in Harold's Cross
Just inside the hall door Drop your luggage on the floor
Throw our arms around each other
And swap a big wet kiss
How the fuck was I going to do this
Knowing that you wouldn't be coming back home again
And I'd be out on me walks
Because my way was always
To think my way around a problem
And I thought And walked And thought And walked further
Still nobody knows I am crying because I'm
Walking the streets in the rain
And sometimes I thought I could walk as far as
Venezuela The Bahamas The Seychelles
But for real this time
It crossed my mind just to walk away
Walk away from the cancer And not have it walking in on top of us
Because I didn't think I'd be able to see it walking away in silence with you
But I knew I couldn't do that either
Knew there was no walking away or way around it
And I knew I'd have to do it And I would of done it
Walk home And when the time came

Just inside the hall door Drop your luggage on the floor
Throw our arms around each other
And swap a big wet kiss
I was going to fuckin do this And show nothing
Knowing you wouldn't be coming back home again
Or that time when the doctor arrived down to us
From the hospice in Harold's Cross on the 23rd of June
And he's asking all his HSE questions
About how much you had paid in St Vincent's
And how much you were earning
And how many rooms did we have
And how much rent we were paying
And his first five questions were all about business And finance
And I'm starting to get a bit cranky
And I said to him
"What's this got to do with anything What's this got to do with her illness"
And he said "Ah nothing Just curious"
And I could see him writing down something
Probably "Husband a bit cranky"
And then he's complaining on about how medicine is too cheap in Pakistan
And about how little money it costs to open a chemist shop there
And I'm getting crankier as you were being polite And I said
"No medicine's the right price in Pakistan The problem is medicine is too expensive here"
And that shut him up for a while
And he's writing down more things probably "Husband more than a bit cranky"
And then he starts going on about God And Heaven
And how great God is
And how happy you're going to be in heaven
And as he's raising his eyes up to heaven
To tell you how happy you're going to be there

I'm looking at you over on your couch beside him
And you're looking back at me on me armchair
And I know our silent expressions are pissed-off listening to him
going on
And thinking 'Get this HSE prick out of here'
And when he finally left And I closed the door after him
And before I could turn around in the hallway you said
"I'm sure God And Heaven are wonderful alright but I like it here
with you"
Because we still had hope then
And we didn't want to be hearing this shite
Because we still had hope then
And later that day Around teatime you said
"Fuck the hospice"
But I can't remember exactly what I said back to you
Maybe I said "Yea fuck the hospice"
But I think maybe I said nothing because I knew that you were going
To have to go up there eventually
A few weeks a few months who knows maybe a few years
Because I didn't want to think about it
Because we still had hope then from day to day
And I had begun to convince meself of the miracle
I'd really started believing in the miracle
Because I didn't want to go to the hospice with you
Just inside the hall door Drop your luggage on the floor
Throw our arms around each other
And swap a big wet kiss
Knowing you wouldn't be coming back home again
But as it turned out On the 6th of August
When the ambulance came to take you away And I was happy
To be going to "Hospital" in an ambulance
The miracle was still on
Because you told me it was a hospital we were going to
"Very clever Very clever My clever little Italian woman"

And that's one time I'm glad you outsmarted me
So I take my small blessings
I take my small blessings
Those little miserable morsels
And I nourish meself on them.

30-September-2009 Arluno

Poem 20

We loved too much Daniela
And that's the problem
Because now I'm thinking
Why couldn't I of married
Some bitter misandrist bitch who I'd grow to despise
Then I wouldn't of given a fuck when she dies
Believe me
There's a lot to be said for it.

1-October-2009 Arluno

Poem 21 – ORA SEMPRE RESISTENZA

I remember that last Tuesday evening The evening before
And I was sitting on me armchair beside your bed resigning meself
And you were knocked out at this stage
And not waking up again
And there was nurses coming in And out
Of your Stella Alpina room
And one of them
One of them Peruvian nurses
Just stood there at the end of your bed for about five minutes
Looking at you sleeping
And I was looking at her
As she just stood there at the end of your bed for about five minutes
And I could see the tears coming to her eyes
And this surprised me
Because it was a hospice
And this was her job for jaysus sake
And there was corpses with the sheets pulled over them
Being wheeled up that corridor every day And night there
You'd think she'd of been used to it by now
Leave her emotions at home
Because this was her job
Because she just stood there at the end of your bed for about five minutes
Looking at you sleeping
And I could see the tears coming to her eyes
And I felt a sort of comfort
Because I knew your spirit of life had touched her.

1-October-2009 Arluno

Poem 22 – DUBLINESE HIBERNO – ENGLISH LESSON

Hi hello wake from thy sleep
God has given your soul to keep
All of the power that burns in the flame
Ignites the light in a single name
Daniela
I was lying in bed last night And I'm still saying to you
"Oiche mhaith" And then I answered for you the way you'd say it
"Oiche mhaith my Seán"
Because I know your speech pattern
Know how you constructed your sentences
Your vocabulary of words Your inflections accent And emphasis
I know how you said things
Even if I didn't always listen to what you said
I always knew how you said them because I loved your
mispronunciations
Like when you used to say "I felt asleep"
You used to ask me to correct you
But usually I never bothered correcting you
And started to talk the same way meself just taking the piss
And I ended up saying things the same way as you without realising it
Or the first year or two you used to be saying to me
"You don't give it a fuckin damn"
Worse than me for repeating yourself
At least I'd usually have the excuse of being drunk for the most of mine
And I left it but after about two years I said it to you one day
"Nobody says that Nobody says "You don't give it a fuckin damn"
except me And you now We're the only two who speak like that"
And you were surprised And you said you'd heard it in a film or a
song And I said "Yea *Gone with the fuckin wind* but nobody talks like that"
'Or it could of been *The Sultans Of Swing* who didn't give it a fuckin
damn about any trumpet playing band either I suppose'
So for once I corrected you And I said to you what you should be saying

In correct Dublinese Hiberno-English is not
"You don't give it a fuckin damn"
It's "You don't give a fuck" or
"You don't give a bollocks" not this
"You don't give it a fuckin damn" stuff
And then after that lesson you always said
"You don't give a fuck" And I always still said Winding you up
"And you don't give it a fuckin damn" And you said
"And you don't give a bollocks" And I'd think
'Pronounced with perfect Dublinese Hiberno-English diction'
Because I know your speech patterns
Know how you constructed your sentences
Your vocabulary of words Your inflections accent And emphasis
I know how you said things
Even if I didn't always listen to what you said
I always knew how you said them because I loved your
mispronunciations
And last night as I was lying in bed
I thought I heard "Seán"
The way you used to say it when you'd come home
When you'd get inside the door wondering where I was
A searching "Seán" like when you were looking for me
It was a very specific emphasis
Said like a question when you'd get home
And I heard that again last night
Exactly the way you used to say it
When you were looking for me
And I remembered after a few seconds where I'd heard it before
The realisation wakening within me just before
I felt asleep.

2-October-2009 Arluno

Poem 23 – HAIKU

LA MIA DANIELA
DOVE SEI
AL PARADISO
SENZA ME.

5-October-2009 Arluno

Poem 24 – THE MEASURE OF MY DREAMS

You'd found me that afternoon in the Seychelles
A May or June bank holiday Monday about seven years ago
And you always knew where to find me
And you walked in And sat down beside me
And I asked you distantly what you were having
And you distantly replied which was our white-flag sign for
CEASEFIRE-NO FIRST STRIKE-WAR IS OVER
But I'd always be relieved And happy when you'd come And find me
But fucked if I was going to show or let you know that
And we usually wouldn't talk too much for a day or two after
Usually but not always
It was more a case of covert surveillance on each other
I'd be watching you when I thought you weren't watching
And I knew you were watching me when you thought I wasn't watching
In the hallway In the kitchen Tight corners
Brush against each other Slight touches
In the bed tipping against each other
Feet Legs Cautiously seeking a response
Accidentally throwing me arm around you in my sleep
And you accidentally in your sleep taking a real tight hold of it
Because usually for a day or two we'd be watching each other
Scrutinising Trying to sound each other out
Mounting psychological observation operations on each other (psych-ops)
A right pair of suspicious short-fused fucks
Trying to gauge To ascertain
Was it still the same between us
But no it was never the same between us
Because it was always more
And you'd found me that bank-holiday Monday afternoon in the
Seychelles
And after a while you started talking
Unusual

And you started crying And you said about how there was only two people
In this world who loved you your father And your mother
And I started to get pissed-off And nearly breaking the ceasefire
And I said "Three Three people Me as well"
And we were nearly having another row about it
And I was telling you to "Stop crying you fuckin sap"
And your tears are bursting into laughter
And I'm proclaiming "Three Three people Me as well I love you as well"
Because after
It was never the same between us
Because after
It was always more.

5-October-2009 Arluno

Poem 25 – WHERE ARE ELMER HERMAN BERT TOM AND CHARLEY AND DANIELA

You gave me that Edgar Lee Masters
Book of poetry as a gift
Antologia di Spoon River-Anthology of Spoon River
This summer two years ago
You wanted me to read it
One page side in English And the other page side in Italian
You thought it would help my Italian
And you said he was your favourite poet
"After you" you were quick to add
And I'd started reading it two summers ago here
And then took it up again last summer here
But I didn't bother reading any of it this summer
Didn't want to be reading about cemeteries
And every grave with a life's story to be told
But I started reading it again last night
Just took it up And started reading it again
Because I know more about cemeteries now
And I'm getting used to the people The dead And the visitors
The dead mostly men The harder life
The visitors mostly old women
Not too many men visiting
And definitely not too many my age
So I'm getting to know all the old women now
There was a time when I just knew all the lads in the bars here
But now I know all the cemetery crowd as well
And I was talking to one old woman last week
And she's saying about how it gets worse after two years
And I had to tell her that I didn't want to know this
"Non voglio di sapere quest"
And she's saying about how every night when she goes to bed
She prays to God that she won't wake up in the morning

And most of all these old women want to do this
Throw themselves on the pyre
And I preferred it when I just knew all the lads in the bars here
But I'm a member of another club now as well
And I can understand when I stand around And listen to their anthologies
About how every night when they go to bed
They pray to God
To rise with death in the morning.

6-October-2009 Arluno

Poem 26 – FOR YOUR LOVE

I was going up to "Il Mercato" this morning
And I stopped to look at that photograph
Of you on the wall at "L'Orologio"
I always stop And look at you
Your big cheeks smiling And your eyes looking straight back at me
You're about four or five years old at
"La Colonnia" summer camp at Varese
Zio Emilio went there one day on his motorbike
And took that photograph of you You told me
And I look at that photograph of you in your cot
When you're about two years old
And you have your arm around that Steiff teddy bear
The exact same way you used to put your arm around me in bed
And you still have that Steiff teddy bear in your bedroom
He's older than me
And every time I go into your bedroom now
I kiss him on the cheeks
And thank him for looking over you when you were little
When I wasn't there
And I look at that photograph of you And your father
You're standing between his knees with your guitar
When you were two and a half years old
I can see Christmassy stuff in the background
And he's sitting over you proudly there
And I feel sort of
Short-changed Cheated
Because I sort of envy him
That he knew you then And I didn't
Because I wish I was the one who'd taken care of you when you were little
I wish I'd of been your father sitting over you proudly there
And then I wish I was your grandfather
I'd of probably spoiled you

And seen my future in your eyes when I'd look at you
And then I wish I was your son
And you'd of taken care of me when I was little
Probably even got me a Steiff teddy bear And a guitar for Christmas
And then I wish I was your grandson
You'd of probably spoiled me
And seen your future in my eyes when you'd look at me
I wish I'd of known you through all those times
Through every possible perspective
I wish I'd of known you through all the generations
Through all the four seasons
And then one more.

7-October-2009 Arluno

Poem 27 – WEDDING DAY – 4th OF JUNE – 2005

I drank three pints of porter in the Seychelles
On me own before the ceremony
Sitting in the corner there just inside the door
Well happy with meself And thinking
'Me getting married Must be some mistake Never thought I'd see the day'
And I'd been making me infallible pronouncements beforehand
We don't need nobody else
"We don't need Church or State telling us what we feel for each other
but fuck it we'll do it anyway"
And I drank three pints of porter in the Seychelles beforehand
On me own just opposite the Oratory in Whitefriar Street Church
And you'd bought a lime-green outfit for four or five hundred euro I think
Good quality Good quality
It had to be Italian knowing you
I never asked or checked the label
Only thought of that now
And I can hardly check it now
Because you only got to wear it twice
Once for our wedding And once for your funeral
Lime green You'd thought about it
Green for Ireland Green for Hope And Green for Luck
And all three of them let you down
When they lowered you down into the ground
In your wedding dress for your funeral
And I was sitting in the Seychelles drinking three pints of porter
In my five euro suit that I'd bought in the Simon charity shop on
Camden Street
'Good quality Good quality '
You warned me off about "Not to be saying that to anybody" (Troppo
tardi adess)
Which I didn't well not really well just a few close confidantes
Sure I was proud of it so I couldn't help boasting a bit

And sure I knew I was only going to be wearing it the once
Don't know what nationality that five euro suit was
Don't know where it is now so I can't check
Because I did only wear it the once
All's I know is that it cost me five euro so it was
Good value Good value
Sitting in the corner there just inside the door
Well happy with meself And thinking
'Three pints of porter Could of nearly bought three suits for meself
with that money'
And it was just over four years later
And Me And Declan And Aidan And Séaghan
Went over to that bar in Bonola shopping centre
And we got what must of been a treble Jack Daniel's
Because it was Daniel'a
And it was over
For you
And you were in the mortuary they were doing you up
And we drank to you Knocked it back in one go
Our Irish way And Irish law
And I said
And they all said
Declan Aidan Séaghan
"Per Daniela For Daniela Salute Sláinte"
And I wasn't even thinking back then
What a widower was
What does that word mean
'Me a widower Must be some mistake Never thought I'd see the day.'

9-October-2009 Arluno

3rd OF JULY 2005 – WHILE OUT CYCLING IN 'IL PARCO DEL ROCCOLO'

This will be the longest summer,
Beginning June the 4th and going on until
The moon somersaults the sun
And the sun crushes its last bead of
Marigold onto our sweating skins,
And then more.
The days, months, years rolling around
Like bicycle wheels going on and on
Past bronze wheat-fields and green corn
That rightly should
But does not envy.
The pathways throwing twinkling surprises
Up into our eyes
The water cascading in the canal
Dashing more to outrun the sun
Although in places pensive and calm
But otherwise strong in its intensity
Tells us that there is no damn
That can hold us back now.
Stopping under the woodland trees for some shade,
Nostrils inhaling flora and fauna,
Simmering contentedly in the interlude
Before pedalling off again, freewheeling.
We will hold onto this
As tightly as we hold onto each other
As tightly as we hold onto the handlebars
Steering us into the future
For this is our "Sentiero", our life long map
For as long as there are summers.

Seán Caomhánach 29-June-05 Via Mazzini 28 Arluno

Poem 28 – IN THE MIDDLE OF THE NIGHT I CALL YOUR NAME "OH DANIELA"

Just never thought you'd die before me Daniela
And you were laughing about four years ago about how it was better for you
Because I'm younger than you
So I'd be able to look after you when you'd be older
I laughed also but doubted it
Because I had planned on you still looking after me
No matter what age you were And you said
"Same age difference between us as between John Lennon And Yoko Ono"
And I said "Yea And John Lennon got whacked"
And now I think how much I'd of had to look forward to
When I'm 64
And you'd be 71
If that situation had of arrived
And you'd be taking the years off your own age
And adding them onto mine instead And I said
"What are you lying about your age for Who gives a fuck"
And of course I'd have to back you up then about it as well
And you'd be adding a year onto my age
And you said "That was the year you were born"
And I said "Yea but I wasn't born 'til December so I won't be that age
until another eleven months" because according to you
Everybody's birthday fell on new years day
Except for your own which was July
Back then I didn't think of it too much
Because I always thought I'd die before you
Even composed a death-bed speech in me head to you once
About how important it was to me
That you continue on with your life
That you don't give up
That's what I'd want for you to be strong

To honour my memory by going on living
Because that's what I'd want
For you to be happy in your life even if I was dead
And all the usual encyclopaedia of clichés
But I've no one to give that speech to now
But at least that was one bit of bullshit
You never had to hear out of me Daniela.

29-October-2009 Arluno

Poem 29

I got you flowers for the balcony for your last birthday with me
I must of known
Because usually I'd get you CD's or some jewellery
But you didn't care once I wrote you a poem for your birthday
And I'd be apologising about the creative quality
And I'd be complaining about the poor poetic standard
And how it wasn't up to much
But you didn't care once I wrote you a poem for your birthday
And you'd always say they were great
But you're not objective
And I must of known
But I'd two thought processes
One short term And the other long term
And I just used the short term day to day one mostly
Just today we live today
And I didn't think of the long term one
Because I was afraid that we didn't have a long term
So I didn't think of it
Just today we live today
But I must of been using my long term thought process
When I got you flowers for the balcony for your last birthday with me
Because I remember that morning in Bonola hospice
That last Friday morning
And you woke up all enthusiastically happy And you said
"Oh I dreamt last night of my beautiful flowers in York Street"
Because I'd got you the flowers And containers for your birthday
And you'd chosen the flowers And planted them yourself in June
Because I didn't know what to get you for your birthday
So I suggested flowers for the balcony
Because I'd wanted something permanent at home
That you'd planted
Something beautiful grown from your hand

That would bloom And bloom after you'd gone
But I never said that exactly or at all
But I think that maybe you understood my practical motivation
But you never said that exactly or at all
Only in Bonola hospice that last Friday morning
When you said you'd dreamed last night
Of your beautiful flowers in York Street
And your beautiful flowers will bloom And bloom again
Because every night on the balcony in York Street
I know they have beautiful dreams of you.

29-October-2009 Arluno

Poem 30 – AIN'T NO SUNSHINE

I walked out in Il Parco del Roccolo two days ago
First time this year I went out there because usually
Every year we'd be here at the beginning of July for your birthday
And on the second day I'd take me bike out from the cellar
And cycle out to Il Parco del Roccolo knowing it was summer
That first sound of my bicycle wheels crunching on the small stones
of the pathway
Told me that summer had arrived And that I had arrived to greet it
And the clear water gushing in the canal
And the colours of green And gold And blue in the sky
And the wheat all bronze in the fields
And the corn all tall And green
And that sweet sticky smell off that plant or tree
Don't know what it's called
But when I'd round that bend on "Sentiero 3"
I could always smell it
And it always smelt of summer And freedom
But I wasn't out there this summer at all
No this summer was just at doctors hospitals a hospice And a funeral
But I walked out in Il Parco del Roccolo two days ago
My heavy shoes crunching on the small stones of the pathway
And the water was drained from the canal
And the sky was slouched in gloom
And there was no corn or wheat in the fields
Just ploughed up clay that fell from the clouds
Just clay in the clouds
And clouds in the clay
And all the same colour of ploughed-up grey
And the trees were bare like plucked upside-down brooms
And that sweet sticky smell off that plant or tree
Don't know what it's called
But I couldn't smell it

Because I could only smell death
And I sat there smoking And thinking at the "Rungia"
Where now there was only death
And I felt real comfortable at home in its midst
And content that this summer was over
Knowing it would never be summer here again.

30-October-2009 Arluno

Poem 31

That last Thursday night in Bonola
It must of been about 9 in the evening in your Stella Alpina room
And the Dottoressa arrived in with the other Dottoressa Clarissa
And a nurse as well
And the Dottoressa was standing at the end of your bed talking
And I understood a good few words
Standing near the door watching And listening
And I understood "Tumore" "Fegato" "Sangue"
But I asked you after they'd left
"What did they mean What were they on about The doctors
I understood "Francamente" but not that bit just after it"
And you said "You know yourself"
And I said "You know yourself what"
And you said "Yes that's what it means You know yourself That's
what she said"
And I said "But what does you know yourself mean"
And you said it meant "You know yourself"
And we were both casual And frank about it
But I didn't really understand what "You know yourself" means
Francamente it took me nearly two days later to know what
"You know yourself" means.

4-November-2009 Arluno

Poem 32

Why should I feel sorry for meself
After what's after happening
It was worse for you
It happened to you not me
And never once did I see you feeling sorry for yourself
You were only sorry to be leaving me
You didn't even want anybody to know
And you were sort of giving out to me in June
Looking at me And you said
"Half of Dublin knows I have cancer And I haven't told anybody"
I said nothing but I just had to keep a low profile for a while But
"Half of Dublin" Daniela
Now that was a bit of an exaggeration.

11-November-2009 Arluno

Poem 33 – RIDERS ON THE STORM

It was always my left hand in your right hand
The imprint of your right hand is still engrained
In my left palm to fingertips
I don't know what to do with it anymore
When I'm out walking
Where I put it
And I remember the first time
I think a Thursday evening around the 16th of September
(Thursday evening the 18th of September I found the ticket when I
got back
You kept it in that pink box in the cupboard I knew you would my
organised woman)
And we were going to see Shane McGowan in Wexford Street
And decided to go to the Swan bar first
A few pints just to relax me
And get me interesting
And we left the old gaff on York Street
And we were crossing the road there
Just at the junction of York And Mercer Streets
And you grabbed my right hand
And I was as embarrassed as fuck
Because it was still bright out
And I thought somebody might see me
Hand in hand with a woman
And I have to live around here you know
And I nervously reacted
Pulled my hand away from you instinctively
And I could see you getting offended
And I didn't want to offend you
And I had to think real quick
Because I knew you were getting offended
And it was our first real night going out together

To see Shane McGowan on Wexford Street
And I didn't want to make a bollocks of things
So I had to think real quick
And I came out with this brilliant bullshit
"No you see because that's me right hand which is me smoking hand
so the other one The left hand is better"
And you being a smoker yourself I knew you'd understand
So after that it was always
My left hand in your right hand
Girl you gotta love your man girl you gotta love your man take him by
the hand make him understand the world on you depends our life can
never end yeah

11-November-2009 Arluno

Poem 34 – THE WEEPING SONG

It was around the beginning of August
And I was sitting in me armchair in the sitting room
Yea I've an Italian armchair in Italy as well you know
Good quality Good quality
And you were on your bed in the bedroom
And you'd turned on Radio Popolare earlier
And Nick Cave came on the radio
So I turned it up And called into you in the bedroom
"Nick Cave is on the radio Daniela"
And you could hear it anyway
And he was singing *The Weeping Song*
And I was singing along to it
And I think you were as well
The way you used to sing it in your best deep voice
This is the weeping song
And I was thinking to meself
'The next time I hear this song I will know its significance'
Because I remember sort of slightly thinking that you may not be here
The next time I hear it
And I was sitting in the same armchair two mornings ago
Listening to Radio Popolare
And Nick Cave came on the radio
And he was singing *The Weeping Song* again
And I thought to meself 'No I was fuckin right'
Because it was the first time I'd heard that song since the last time
And I knew its significance
Because you weren't on your bed in the bedroom anymore
And there was nobody there that I could call into And say
"Nick Cave is on the radio"
Because Nick Cave was on the radio
Weeping for you Daniela.

12-November-2009 Arluno

Poem 35 – CHE CAZZO È LA STORIA DANIELA

Che cazzo è la storia Daniela
Because you've appeared in Nina's dreams
In good form telling her how well you're keeping
And then I was talking to Laura today
And she's telling me that two nights ago
You appeared in her dream as well
All smiling And in great form
And you threw your arms around her
And the two of youse had a laugh Ed un grande abbraccio
And then there's others saying also
That you've been visiting them in their dreams at night
And you're always in great form Having a laugh
You seem to be living a very hectic night-life these days
From what I'm hearing
Out gallivanting 'til all hours
Dropping into friends in their dreams
Smiling Joking Socialising with them
And seemingly enjoying yourself by all accounts And appearances So
Che cazzo è la storia Daniela
Because I can remember three dreams I've had of you
And in all three dreams you've been dead
And in these dreams
I've known that you're dead
And I've woke up in the morning
Knowing that you're dead
And I've gone to bed at night
Knowing that you're dead
My dreams are dead Daniela.

14-November-2009 Arluno

Poem 36

It was just over four years ago
And we were sitting outside Bar Filippo-Il Gallo
On a Sunday morning
And I was there in me shorts And sandals
Taking a tan on me toes
And drinking a bottle of beer
When that big mad bastard with the tattoos on his neck
Mauro "Budha" arrived And he's pissed drunk already
And he's singing that Smiths song
Good times for a change please please please let me let me let me
And we just joined in And sang along with him
And then started laughing
And you were impressed that "Budha"
Knew all the words to the song
And because of it you became impressed with him
Because before that you didn't really like him so much
But after yea you were impressed that he
Knew all the words to the song
And why would a big mad bastard like him
With the tattoos on his neck be singing a song like that in the first place
And I was walking down Il Corso sta mattina
And I met "Budha" on it
And the big mad bastard threw his arms around me
And as he's asking me "Come stai"
I just started singing to him
And he joined in because he
Knew all the words to the song
Good times for a change You see the luck that I've had can make a
good man turn bad
And we sang the song And laughed
Because the life that I've had can make a good man bad
So we sang a duet to you And laughed instead.

16-November-2009 Arluno

Poem 37

Remember the way I used to talk to meself Daniela
And you'd say "What did you say"
And I'd say "I'm just talking to meself"
And then after a while when I was just talking to meself
And you said "Ah you're just talking to yourself si"
And I said "Si just talking to meself A private conversation Don't be earwigging"
And you said "Don't be what"
And I said "Ah you don't listen to me"
You wouldn't know if I was serious or not
I suppose I can tell you now Daniela
Neither would I
But I'm back in the gaff in Dublin two days now
And I've given up the talking to meself now
I don't do it anymore now
Because instead I just talk to you all the time now.

20-November-2009 York Street

Poem 38 – IN THIS PLACE

In this place filled with empty space
Your love holds the key baby sympathise with me
I need you before I lost your touch of life and grace
I knew that your sweet face could always comfort me
Back home permanent In This Place three days now Daniela
I was back a couple of times since August
But they were just coming And going never staying long or settling
But now I have to settle
Settle in here without you
It's strange not seeing you not hearing you
Not feeling your presence in the gaff
I've imagined you on your couch
In the hallway In the kitchen Tight corners
Brush against each other Slight touches
In the bed tipping against each other
Feet Legs Just mine
Strained to hear your voice
I'm trying to forget the bad times
Since we moved in here on the 6th of April
When you were up all night all May And June sick
Restless in bed
Then sitting at the table in the chair in the kitchen in the dark
Now even those times seem like good times
They won't leave me
Even if I'm leaving everything in the gaff
Exactly as it was when we left for three weeks holidays
In Italy on the 1st of July
You'd probably laugh And say that's because I'm a lazy man
Too much effort changing things
But that's not my reason
I just can't won't change
Haven't even bothered changing the calendars

Although for the time change at the end of October
I did have to put the clock back an hour
Wishing I could of put it back twelve years.

21-November-2009 York Street

Poem 39 – SCRAMBLED EGGS

I cooked up the scrambled eggs for meself
Yesterday
First time in over six months since I'd done that
You used to love my scrambled eggs on toast
Knew by the way you used eat them
Head down Full of concentration
You even ate the exact same way as Pasquale
I used to look at you eating the scrambled eggs
Laughing Slagging you off about Pasquale
But you wouldn't allow any distractions
Apart from doing your Homer Simpson impression
Knowing you really enjoyed them
My Saturday lunchtime speciality
Or sometimes my other culinary speciality
Of beans on toast with a poached egg
Scooping the bowl of beans spreading them like stars
But I know you preferred my scrambled eggs
Cooked them just for you in May And June as well
Just the eggs don't bother with the toast
Because scrambled eggs are light
But you weren't really enjoying them anymore
Because they wouldn't go down your throat stay down
Kept coming up
You tried but they wouldn't go down your throat stay down
So I didn't bother cooking them anymore Until
Yesterday
They stayed down for me
But you kept coming up
I can't even eat scrambled eggs now
Without thinking about you.

24-November-2009 York Street

Poem 40 – "BONOLA FERMATA BONOLA" 6-August-09

"Bonola Fermata Bonola"
How many times did we hear that over the trains "Public Address"
When we'd be going in And out of Milan on the Metro
And it meant nothing to us
"Bonola Fermata Bonola"
But yea
Our train stopped at Bonola
Cristo si è fermato a Bonola
And it's exactly four months ago now today Daniela
And I was thinking of that last Thursday
The 6th of August when we went to Bonola
And that afternoon when I still thought it was a hospital
And you were in your bed doing your leg exercises
Bed cycling like your hero Fausto Coppi
And you were able to cycle your legs
And seemed to be getting the strength back into them
And you hadn't been able to do anything like that in weeks
And I thought you were getting your physical strength back
And I said enthusiastically to you
"Look You see We're only in here a few hours And you're getting
better already"
And I said it with conviction
Because I believed what I said then
And later that evening we were talking
And you came out with another one of your proclamations
"I'm not afraid of dying I'm only afraid of leaving you..."
And then you hesitated a bit And you said
"I'd be jealous...Jealous of other women"
I said nothing but I thought
'At last you admit it After nearly twelve years you admit it I knew it
I was fuckin right all along'
But I didn't feel like jumping up on your bed

Doing a victory dance on it And cheering
"Yes I was fuckin right all along"
Because I was happy that the strength
Seemed to be returning to your legs
And on top of that the return of your jealousy
Must mean that you were getting back to normal again
That's how I interpreted it
Another sign that you were getting back to normal again
And I said nothing
Just sitting there listening
And you said
"I'll haunt you"
And you started laughing And then you said
"Only a joke"
And I was thinking 'Yea like fuck it is as if you'd make a joke about a
thing like that'
But you can haunt me anytime you want Daniela
But so far its just been imaginary
A wind blowing into the corner of me eye
And I turn to see but it's only a tree or a lamppost
Or I look down the dark hallway from me armchair
And sit up then expecting to see
But it's only the blackness materialising because
I WANT TO SEE YOUR FACE AGAIN
I get up during the night
And look around the corner into the kitchen
Thinking you might be sitting there like you were
Last May And June sick
And I still say to you anyway
"Come on to bed Daniela"
But you're not there
So I sit at the table in the chair in the kitchen in the dark
Where you used to sit smoking And thinking
Now I sit there also smoking And thinking

But how can I think what you must of thought
Although I do try
But you must of known that I never wanted to know
About the future
I fought it like you fought it
Right up 'til the present was nearly over
I shielded meself with disbelief
You know why Daniela
You know this.

12-December-2009 York Street

Poem 41 – *I* (DON'T) *WANNA BE SEDATED*

One of the doctors told me that last Friday evening
Half-English half Italian we were talking
She told me that you did not want to be sedated
It was the first I'd heard of it
But I never said anything to you about it
Because I knew you wanted to take death on
Show it you had no fear
But when the doctor told me that you'd said
You didn't wanna be sedated
I nearly fuckin laughed
Because I was thinking of The Ramones
And I would of been sure that Joey Ramone
Would of answered that question about sedation for you
And that when they asked you that question
You would of started singing straight away
I wanna be sedated
Because how many times did you see The Ramones live
And how many films documentaries of The Ramones had you seen
And how many records videos bootlegs t-shirts of The Ramones did
you have
And how many times would you be dancing And singing around the gaff
While The Ramones blasted
And I'd be sitting on me armchair
And you'd be dancing And singing right up into my face
I wanna be sedated or that other one
I wanna live
And when you danced And sang it
I knew you meant it
And I'd be sitting on me armchair
Doing me best to be unmoved And I said
"I can't see the fuckin telly with you Can't hear it either"
On account of you and Joey Ramone doing your duet on

I wanna be sedated
Because that's what came to my mind immediately
You dancing And singing around the gaff
Like Chief Crazy Woman
When the doctor told me that you said
"I don't wanna be sedated"
Because I was thinking that you just couldn't of helped yourself
And that when they asked you that question
You would of started singing straight away
I wanna be sedated
But the doctor told me they were going to sedate you anyway
Because the doctor told me the tumour had spread from your pancreas
Into your liver And was moving in for the kill
And cancerous blood was travelling from your liver towards your
stomach
And when it got there
You'd of had a massive seizure
A breathing fit that would of violently strangled you
And you'd of died roaring
Roaring a duet with Joey Ramone
I wanna be sedated.

12-December-2009 York Street

Poem 42 – HOW I DISCOVERED THE WASHING MACHINE

You wouldn't believe it Daniela
Eventually got around to working
Your Zanussi Italian washing machine today
More or less had to
Couldn't crush any more dirty clothes into the washing basket
But some of them are yours
Two pairs of jeans a bra socks
And the bonus
Don't know what I'll do with them
Washed them alright but won't be ironing them
Just put them in one of your many wardrobes with the rest of your things
All your beautiful things Daniela
All your beautiful things
I don't know what to do with them all
So I won't do nothing
Just leave everything the way you left it
Won't be ironing anything
Ironing is finished here
But your Italian washing machine seemed very complicated
Loads of buttons on it
Just started pressing them And see what happens
On my fourth washing load now
More or less have the hang of it
The first one wasn't great though
Discovered where to put the washing-powder
And pressed a few buttons
But that sky blue towel is now purple
Coincidentally the exact same colour of purple
As that purple sheet I put in the wash with it
But I'm learning
Won't make that mistake again
Because I've also discovered the "Colour-catchers" now

Because I've also discovered that your Italian washing machine
Isn't very complicated at all
Once you get the hang of it
As a matter of fact
I think I'm becoming addicted to it
All them buttons technology science
I'm inclined to agree with my mother now
Because she always says
That the washing machine was the greatest discovery of all time
I'm inclined to agree
Because I find it fascinating now
Watching it spin around
All the temperatures spins cottons daily synthetics wool delicates
Pre-wash super pre-wash intensive extra-quick
The washing powder That stuff for the wool The fabric conditioner hmm
But the greatest discovery was the colour-catchers which I discovered
In the closet in the hall
Can't really recall looking in there before
Can't really recall looking in all them other cupboards before either
But I have to now
I'm discovering every day
And I have to use the washing machine
But I'm enjoying it
Can't wait for the next wash
I hope its not just a case of the novelty wearing off
It's compulsive
It appeals to my nature
I can understand its addiction
And that's an addiction you deprived me of
For all those years with you doing the washing
But I can understand why you hogged it all for yourself
And I'm keeping the gaff fairly clean in general also
Sweeping And dusting
Usually mop the floors every Saturday

I'm not as meticulous And organised as you
But I'm doing alright
It's not like there's empty cans of beer
Overflowing out of the bin or that (well only exceptionally occasionally)
It's not like the gaff is in bits which might surprise you
I'm doing me best
Takes time to get organised
And I'll never be as organised as you
Because you used to even say yourself
That maybe there was a bit of an Austrian in you
Way back along the genetic line
And you didn't like the Austrians
You didn't much like any of the Europeans
Except for the French
Because you'd always say "Ah the French know how to do a strike"
Except for the Serbs
They always had one faithful heart with you
I don't know why
Or maybe I do
World War 2
And you'd say
"Up the Serbs Up the Serbs"
With your left fist clenched
That always made me laugh
And you said to me once some other story
Can't remember exactly what it was
Then you said
"I'm funny I'm funny"
I wasn't saying anything
But you pressurised me
"I'm funny I'm funny"
Then I said "Yea sort of"
Maybe I didn't like the idea
Of you encroaching on my territory

I'm the comedian around here
But I will tell you what always made me laugh was
"Up the Serbs Up the Serbs"
With your left fist clenched
I couldn't help meself
Up the ante Up the ante
But I'm not making a show of you
Most of the time
Or you wouldn't be ashamed of me
Or letting meself or the gaff go to pieces
Although I probably wouldn't notice if I was
But I'm getting there slowly
I'm even getting into the cooking of pasta
Like you used to say to people
"Put a plate of spaghetti in front of Seán everyday And he'll eat it"
I put plates of spaghetti in front of meself nearly every day now And
I'm eating them
Building up my repertoire of pasta recipes
Got a few from Antonello
Carbonara Pasta al Ragù
And Aidan gave me a book on cooking pasta
So I can cook that tomato "Sugo" sauce that you used to do now
And to tell you the truth
I think my Irish tomato "Sugo" sauce is more tasty than yours
But I'd still prefer yours
Because you were too rigid on your rules of Italian cooking
Whereas me I like to experiment
And I'm putting garlic into the sugo
It says to put garlic into the sugo in the book
Just as well you never seen that book or you'd go berserk
But do you know what a "Shallot" is Daniela
Neither did I
So I had to google it
In case I went out and bought the wrong thing

But I know all about shallots now
It says about shallots in the book
And I was reading it thinking
'What the fuck is a shallot'
So I had to google it
It turns out that a "Shallot" is an "Onion" A fuckin onion
So I'm putting shallots into the tomato sauce
You wouldn't approve
And I agree
Because why didn't the book just say an "Onion"
Instead of this fuckin pretentious shite about shallots
That I had to google
It's just as well you didn't send me out for a "Shallot" that day years ago
When you sent me out for the onion
Or I'd of never of come home
Be still out walking around looking for it
And wondering what it was
Because we didn't have the internet back then
Because before
A "Shallot" had as much significance for me as what a "Colour-
catcher" did
I'd of thought that a colour-catcher
Was some sort of trendy psychedelic dance drug
Until I discovered them in the closet in the hall
Me and Cristoforo Colombo The Great Discoverers
Like they were never there before
I'm like Colombus
"What about Saint Brendan"
I discovered the washing machine And the colour -catchers
Me mammy is very grateful to me
But really all's that Colombus discovered was the sea
Like it was never there before
He didn't even make his own boat
Or dye his own sail with a purple sheet And purple towel

Like what I did
But we agreed on that about "Chief" Crazy Horse was there before
Amerigo Vespucci
But we agreed on just about everything
Although that wouldn't necessarily stop us from arguing
Over some finer point about it
Because you were my "Injun" Chief Crazy Woman
No one else could of lived with me
No one else could of lived with you
'til death do us part
Death
You think we part
Mai
Yea Colombus discovered the colour-catchers
And I know what is true
But I've heard all this before about how
It was an Italian who discovered the telephone
But his patent was robbed (Meucci)
And it was an Italian who invented the first suspension bridge
And it was an Italian who discovered Art
And it was an Italian who discovered Culture
And you don't have to keep going on all the time about
What a fuckin genius Leonardo Di Vinci was And all his discoveries
Non mi interessa
"What about Saint Brendan"
Because all's I'm interested in knowing is that
It was an Italian who discovered
Me.

25-November-2009 And 24-March-2010 York Street

Poem 43 – QUESTA OFFESA DEVE ESSERE LAVATA COL INCHIOSTRO

-"You get it for me"-"Give me fifteen minutes"-"Don't let anybody in"-"I love you too"-
"What's going on"- "I try to get up"-"Yea"-"5 minutes"- "Are you sure I'll be fine" "quarto d'ora minuti"
That last Saturday afternoon in Bonola.
The 8th of August.
I knew it was over.
Finally I knew it was over.
Knew there was no hope left.
Finally I'd realised it.
Knew you were fucked.
No hope for you.
No miracle.
Just death.
Just a matter of a short time.
Didn't want to know it.
Never wanted to know it.
Had spent a year And a half determined not to know it.
Kept telling you that you'd be fine. (Because you're mine Because you're mine.)
Think I convinced you of it.
Think I convinced you of it because I know I convinced meself of it.
It was all lies And bullshit.
That last Saturday afternoon I knew it.
Was sure of it.
Finally it had sunk in.
It was over.
I thought you were going to die that night.
No hope And No miracle.
On the 11th of July at home the day after you were discharged from Humanitas hospital

And you said "The cancer sleeps."
And I said "Sleeps."
And you said "Dorme."
And I said "Dormant."
I thought about that all day.
Whispered it to meself.
Whispered it because I didn't want to wake it up.
"It's dormant."
The miracle is starting to happen.
All day I whispered it to meself.
"Fuckin dormant."
Even drank a few cans that night in the gaff to embellish my optimism.
I relaxed a bit And felt good.
I'd given up on medicine And science.
Then we went to that IOE institute in Milan around the 20th of July.
The top oncologist in Italy.
(Apart from advising you to smoke a bit of marijuana for munchies
to help your appetite he said he'd try a new experimental treatment
on you when you got some strength back.
I said to you after "This bloke charges you 250 euro to tell you to smoke
a bit of blow for your appetite. I could of told you that for nothing.")
And I went into the Church near the institute that morning.
Lit a candle for you.
The Church was called the "Church Of Miracles."
It was all starting to make sense.
Everything was fitting in And adding up.
Get you into Bonola "Hospital".
Get your "Peristalsis" sorted out And who knows.
A miracle.
Maybe you'd last 'til October I was thinking.
Maybe Christmas.
Maybe a year.
Maybe two years.
Yea we can do a lot of things in two years.

Who knows.
But I knew that last Saturday afternoon in Bonola.
No fuckin miracle.
No fuckin hope.
Just fuckin death.
Inevitable And Unstoppable.
I wrote down your words.
Just a few snippets of them.
You were lapsing in And out of it
I wanted to remember your last words to me.
Morbid.
It had finally sunken in.
That afternoon.
All my friends.
San Antonio San Pellegrino San Francesco San Pio.
My dead granny My dead daddy.
None of them done nothing for you.
I didn't want to believe.
It was over.
I knew it.
And now I wanted it over as quick as possible.
Get it over with.
And I was on the smoking terrace smoking And thinking.
It was 40 degrees And I could feel every one of them burning me up inside.
Thinking 'It's over.'
That's it.
No more.
It's fuckin finished.
Had to face it.
Didn't want to face it.
Never wanted to face it.
But now I had to face what you were facing.
Facing what was facing you.
Because now it was happening.

The end was happening.
I knew it.
And I could feel meself cracking.
Didn't know what to do.
Wanted to get away.
Didn't want to deal with it.
I wanted it over now.
Would of smothered you meself just to get it over with.
But you would of fought me.
Besides they told me they were going to sedate you.
Told me you'd said that you didn't wanna be sedated.
But they were going to do it anyway.
I said ok.
Va ben.
Didn't say anything to you about it
But I knew.
I fuckin knew alright.
Knew it was over.
And I was sitting on the smoking terrace smoking And thinking.
40 degrees.
Hadn't slept properly in months.
The stress.
I wanted to get away from the reality.
I'd of smothered you meself if I thought it was any use.
You were getting killed anyway.
I could kill.
Somebody.
Deliver me my vengeance.
It might of helped.
Me.
No.
Because you would of fought me anyway.
You fought all the way.
All fight.

When the doctor even said to me in the hospice about your heart
And head staying strong.
But your body was crumbling.
Breaking down.
They said you were fighting it.
They said you were tough.
'I know I'm married to her.'
But I'd all this rage inside of me And no place for it to go.
And I wanted to go.
Give me something.
Bang something into me.
Some of that stuff they were injecting into you.
I did wanna be sedated.
Send me off sleeping to.
Venezuela The Bahamas The Seychelles.
Because I knew I was cracking.
Knew it was getting to me.
Getting too much.
Deliver me my vengeance for you.
Profondo nel mio cuore sono un terrone.
But I knew you needed me.
For a little while longer anyway.
I couldn't crack.
Too easy of a cop-out.
But I wasn't sure if I could control it.
Everything was like your body.
Everything was crumbling.
Everything was breaking down.

25-November-2009

....
I was breaking down.
I knew it.

Sitting on the smoking terrace smoking And thinking.
Couldn't put it off any longer.
Had to face what you were facing.
You were fucked.
And then your fuckin mother came out onto the smoking terrace.
Doesn't even smoke what was she doing on it.
I was sitting haunched over on the chair.
Fuckin wired up.
She was standing over me.
Wasn't listening to her.
I was just smoking And thinking.
It's over.
All the bullshit I told meself.
It all ends today.
Never thought this would happen.
I was told it would happen.
Knew all the medical scientific facts.
But never really believed them.
I had hope.
Hope was dying in your body.
I always had hope.
Fuck all else.
I needed it.
And your fuckin mother is standing over me shiteing out of her.
Must of ignored her for at least five minutes.
Wasn't listening.
Couldn't hear her.
You know that irritating nutcase way she has of going on.
Your fuckin mother.
The fuckin mother of all fuckin mothers in law.
I just wanted to be left alone.
In peace.
Not your fuckin mother in me ear.
Not now.

But she wouldn't let it go.

I don't know what she was on about.

I wasn't listening.

I was smoking And thinking.

And after about five minutes.

Or maybe ten minutes.

Or maybe two.

I just snapped.

Exploded.

It had a place to go.

……………………………………

It all began over a priest.

I'd said to her that morning that maybe we ought to get you a priest.

I wanted to be sure that you were safe.

I was hoping I'd see you again.

That it wasn't over.

I believed it at that time.

I had to believe something.

I was desperate.

When the music's over.

I was thinking Hendrix Jimi Hendrix as well.

And if I don't meet you no more in this world I'll meet you in the next one don't be late don't be late.

And I knew she only disagreed with it because it was my idea.

My suggestion.

If she'd of thought of it it would of been a great idea.

She wouldn't of even bothered asking me about it.

Always control.

No wonder you got away from her.

I knew you were a good communist.

I knew you were a Catholic.

Cattocomunista.

Loads of them in Italy.

Take their religion from Rome but not their politics.

I asked you.

When I was filling in the census form years ago.

I asked you.

Turned around from the table where I was filling it in And I said.

"A question here Daniela what religion are we."

And you said "Catholic we're Catholic."

What the fuck did your fuckin mother know.

We were down in Clonfert at the end of January.

Up the St. Peregrine centre in Rathfarnham in June.

You'd take communion when you were getting the chemo in St. Vincent's.

Saying your novenas in bed at night.

I'd be rubbing that Lourdes holy water into your side where you were soring.

One night you said it worked.

Think I even convinced meself that I could cure you.

All your angels And holy pictures And holy medals.

All for nothing.

But we were desperate.

What the fuck did your fuckin mother know.

"And if I don't meet no more in this world I'll meet you in the next one don't be late don't be late."

You have to believe in something.

We'd try everything.

And that's how it started.

The priest.

I wanted to be sure.

Wanted you to live forever.

That's what I meant when you asked me "Are you sure I'll be fine."

I wasn't thinking about this world when I said "Yea you'll be fine."

I wanted to be sure for you.

I'm sure for you but I'm not so sure about me.

I'm not so sure about anything anymore.

And your fuckin interfering controlling nutcase fuckin mother.

Standing over me mouthing off.

She must of been there for about five or ten minutes.
I just snapped.
Exploded.
It had a place to go
And what snapped me into it was her roaring at me And pointing
her finger
"Tu stai zitto"
Me shut up
I wasn't even listening to her never mind talking
And I'm getting up from the chair
And fuck your fuckin mother I'm getting a fuckin priest
"No tu stai zitta"
And then she's roaring at me
"Tu sei pazzo"
And I'm roaring back
"No tu sei pazza"
And after that it just took off
All sorts of shit
And I was sorry I couldn't speak better Italian
So as I could curse And swear more at her
And tell her what I really thought of her
So I had to do some of it in English
I'd say she understood though
And all the patients And visitors on the smoking terrace were
Staring at us
And all the doctors And nurses standing inside the glass door were
Staring at us
I didn't give a fuck
Was sorry I couldn't express
Some of the things you'd said to me about her
Mournful fuckin mother my bollocks
When the shows over so are her tears
Avrebbe preferito un cane
And we're roaring at each other on the smoking terrace

A big audience watching
In this place of peace And tranquillity for the dying
Fuck that
And I had to get away from her
Because the smoking terrace just overlooked the mortuary
Too much temptation just to throw her overboard the railings into it
(I coccodrilli)
(The mortuary even had an advertising sign touting for business
On the lamppost just in front of the smoking terrace
Publicising the different burials cremations vestments they had
So as you were there having your smoke
You could make your choice
Very considerate but I think it was just bad taste)
And I stormed in through the automatic glass door
Into the hospice
Through all the doctors And nurses gathered inside it
Didn't look at any of them
Just head down And cut straight through them all
I'd say they won't forget the Irishman
They had in Bonola hospice for six forty degree hot days And nights
In August this year for a long time
And I stormed down the corridor to your Stella Alpina room
And you were asleep And I started shouting at you
"That fuckin mother of yours is driving me fuckin nuts"
And you were still asleep
You must of heard me
But I wanted to shake And wake you up to tell you
I was going to wake you up to tell you
Because I knew you would of understood
You would of backed me up
And I wanted to talk to you And tell you about
The petty problems of the living
But I decided against it
Because you were sleeping

Because you were dying
So I couldn't
And you were dying
And I sat down beside your bed
And I knew I was losing it
But you were sleeping And dying
I'd no one to talk to
No one to understand
Sure you were facing death
So I just sat there knowing
That you were dying
And I was cracking
No way back

26-11-2009
…………………………………
I'd said to you earlier at lunchtime about the priest
Real casual
Always careful with my words to you
I said a Saturday evening
Probably be a priest around
Doing his normal rounds
No big deal
Not specifically for you
I'd already asked for one
You said "Yea" And I knew by the way you said "Yea"
That it was a "Yea"
And you said to me "You get it for me" the communion
Just in case you felt asleep
"Give me fifteen minutes"
You wanted to sleep for fifteen minutes but you couldn't
All restless
Sitting up Lying down Sitting up Lying down
"I try to get up"

That was the cancer kicking in
Moving in for the kill
"Don't let anybody in"
(Yea especially your fuckin mother)
I said I'd get the communion for you if were asleep
Hadn't got it since we got married
Next time I got it was at your funeral
But you'd got it in St. Vincent's when you were getting the chemo out there
And also when we went down to Clonfert with Shane last January
Looking for a miracle
And when we went to the St. Peregrine centre in Rathfarnham
You'd taken communion
And I found a load of religious memorabilia of yours
Since I came back to the gaff in York Street
In your pockets And drawers
Alongside your Che Guevara And Lenin stuff
Some communist you are Some communist you are
Cattocomunista
We don't take our politics from Rome
"What's going on"
You were dying that's what was going on
"I try to get up"
You couldn't
"Are you sure I'll be fine"
"Yea you'll be fine"
I didn't say where though
And you said to me
"I love you too"
So I must of said it first

....
Your fuckin mother came back into your room
After the row After a while
L'erba grama non muore mai
Doing her usual fuckin victim

"Fai la vittima"
You were her corpse
Nearly
Her public display of great care
A bit late for that now
And she's sitting on the other side of your bed
And you're still sleeping
And I started it up again
She started it the first time
Now I was going to continue it
I wouldn't let it go
Fuck her And her fuckin orders
Your fuckin mother disrupts my peace
So I'll disrupt hers
She gets it back She gets it back
And she's patrolling around your bed And I said
"Tu stai zitta"
And we were back at it again
Then a doctor And nurse came in
Must of heard us
Broke it up
Had to call a halt
I went out
Doctor was doing the mediator
Your fuckin mother was on about where you were going to be buried
That's what it was all about
Nothing got to do with the priest
She seemed to resent the idea that I might have some say in the matter
I said ok here is fine
Once we're buried together
It was always supposed to be in Dublin with Daddy
That's what we'd said pre-cancer years ago
I made a mistake
Especially when your fuckin mother menaces me in October

Saying I wasn't going to be buried with you
No I was going to be buried on me own in Ireland
No Kavanaghs in Arluno ever again
According to her
With that fuckin smirk on both her fuckin faces
Who the fuck does she think she is
It didn't matter where
Once we're buried together
The doctor brokered a sort of agreement later
She was sitting on the other side of your bed with her sun-glasses on her
My head was going
You were sleeping
Kevin texted me saying him And Shane could make it over the
next morning
I texted back "Yea"
And Declan rang me after I'd texted him saying
"I think I'm cracking up"
And he asked me "Promise me you won't do anything"
I couldn't promise so I just told him
"I won't talk to her I won't even look at her but if she says anything to
me she's getting it back"
And he said him And Aidan were coming over on Monday
I needed my family
And you woke up in the evening
Just after peace broke out
We put on a show for you Daniela
A happy family show
But you must of heard the row
But we put on a show
Of course your fuckin mother was far better at it then me
Far more experience at being a phoney
She started talking across the bed to me "Mangi"
No I hadn't eaten couldn't eat
But she stayed late that night

'til about ten
She usually left at eight
Except for the last two nights when she stayed
It was too late for a priest
But I was getting one the next morning
And fuck your fuckin mother
That's if you were still alive
She went off about ten
Gave her a kiss on the cheek
And let it go
Settled in for the night
Dimmed the light
I thought you'd die at night
Sat on me armchair
Yea I'd an armchair in the hospice as well
Feet up on your bed beside your basin
On the alert as the vomit-catcher
You were throwing up that night in between sleeping
And it came to about 6am on the Sunday morning
Always liked that time there
Just before dawn but still dark
But light beginning to seep through
Always loved that time in the hospice
Felt at peace
You'd made it
Always thought you'd die at night
There was a full moon
And it had moved 45degrees since the Saturday night
And it was directly over the church now
I stood on the smoking terrace watching it
Watching the light dissipate the dark
Watching the blueing sky envelope the moon behind it
Just sort of cusped it And swallowed it down
I watched the entire movement

Never saw that happening before
The way the blue sky just nudged its way around it
And poked it into its pocket
And I said "Good-bye mister moon The next time I see you I'll know
what its going to feel like to be there all alone on your own like you"
And it just disappeared
Behind the blue sky
And I thought of my dead father
Some old poem he learned the short time he was in school
He used to always recite a few lines
"Don't care don't care don't care he shattered out with glee"
And I said to the moon
"Don't care don't care don't care I shattered out with glee"
And I could feel the insanity lifting
Disappearing behind the blue sky
Or maybe it didn't
It didn't matter
I knew I could get through it
Knew I'd be there for you
Knew I'd found the strength
And I got onto the nurse about the priest
Your mother was coming in to do relief at 10am
As I'd to go And meet Kevin And Shane at Centrale at about noon
And Declan And Aidan were arriving on Monday
I knew I could handle it
And I got onto the nurse
And she said she couldn't get a priest 'til the night
Would that be ok
I just looked at her
Waved me hand down towards your room without saying nothing
But as if to say "Well what the fuck do you think"
So she rang again And got a priest from "Our lady queen of peace church"
Can't remember his name but he didn't look like a priest
And Julio the nurse called me

"Il prete è qui"
But I was looking for him
Because he looked more like a DJ
I warned him off "Sotto voce" And went into you And I said
"There's a priest here just doing his normal Sunday rounds And he
wants to give us a blessing"
And you said "Yea"
I don't think you believed me about the "Blessing" bit
I know now you knew it was "The last rites"
No you said "Si"
Because I remember the way you jumped back on your bed
Like a little girl
I see that now in my mind a lot like I see those tears in the ambulance
Like I see you sitting at the table in the chair in the kitchen in the dark
Last May And June sick
Where now I sit at the table in the chair in the kitchen in the dark
And you wouldn't be in bed
So I'd get up
And you'd be sitting here with your head down
Smoking And thinking And trying to drink one of those "Fresubin" drinks
But they wouldn't go down your throat stay down And I'd say to you
"Come on to bed Daniela"
And I didn't want to be nagging you
So I'd leave it And go back to bed
Wondering what the fuck must be going on in your head
Then you answered all the prayers in Italian
Then you said a bit extra in at the end
And the priest I think he said that extra bit was only for
confirmation cresimo
You'd remembered it from then
And I saw the priest out the door And thanked him
You knew fuckin well it was "The last rites"
And me bullshitting about a "Blessing"
But after you were happy about it

Or as happy as you can be about receiving "The last rites"
And I kissed you And said I was going out for a walk
And I was happy about it
Or as happy as I could be about you receiving "The last rites"
There was nothing more I could do for you now except
just Waiting
And I kissed you thinking
And if I don't meet you no more in this world I'll meet you in the next one
don't be late don't be late
And I met your mother And Luciano in the corridor arriving
And I kissed her And told her I was going to meet my brother Kevin
He's here for me (I didn't mention about Shane)
Because Declan had said to me in late July
That you said to Kevin around last March you said
"I'm not afraid of dying I'm only worried about Seán"
And I only heard this at the end of July
So I knew that I didn't need her "permission"
"È qui per me Daniela l'ha detto"
I knew that's what you wanted
You knew that's what I wanted before I knew I wanted it My
Very clever Very clever little Italian woman
And I took the red-line from Bonola to Cadorna
And the green-line from Cadorna to Centrale
And I met Kevin And Shane outside it
It wasn't even midday
And it was already 34degrees
But I knew I could handle that heat
Sunday mornings always peaceful
And I knew there wouldn't be no *Bad Moon Rising* again for
another month
And I was sure I could handle the sun.

28-November-2009 York Street

Poem 44 – 3rd OF JULY 2009 – HUMANITAS HOSPITAL – ROZZANO

I found that last birthday card I got you last night
In a bag in the cupboard with the rest of your birthday cards
I'm finding things in the gaff all the time now
And I remember that day
Your last birthday in Humanitas hospital in Rozzano
You wanted to sit in the sun
So I wheeled you out in your wheelchair with your "Flebo" drip
To the garden at the front of the hospital
And it was a real hot 3rd of July
And you were dehydrated
And I was afraid that if you sat in the sun for too long
You might only evaporate
But you wanted to sit in the sun for a while
Unusual because usually you preferred in the shade
So after a while we sat in the shade just talking
Even talked about the future
For once we talked about the future And you said
"We'll go back to Paris in September"
And I said
"Yea we'll go back to Paris in September"
The only time we talked about or made plans for the future
And we sat there just talking that day
In the garden at the front of the hospital
For our last birthday together
And I bought a prosciuto And bree toasted roll And a bottle of sprite
In the restaurant across the road
And you got a mint ghiacciolo ice-pop for your dehydration
I presume you threw it up after
And later that night you sent me a text message
You mis-spelt a few words
Because you were that weak

You couldn't even work your fingers properly And you texted
"Oiche mhaith.thanks for tie day.buona notte.love you tanto"
That was easy
Kirsty McColl not The Kinks -*Thank you for the day*-That's where
you got it from
And I remember that calm balmy day now
Our last birthday together
Sitting in the shade just talking
And for your birthday again
I'll go And sit in the garden at the front of Humanitas hospital again
Where we sat this year And I'll wish you
"Tanti auguri a te e buon compleanno"
It all seemed so peaceful
So far away
And I'll read me poems to you
And we'll talk again
About going back to Paris in September.

13-December-2009 York Street

3rd OF JULY – 2009 – HUMANITAS HOSPITAL – ROZZANO

The third of July again and the sun beaming
Like the big smile always across your face
So it doesn't matter where we are
Be it sitting on the grass at The Eiffel Tower,
Or Petit Bar, or waiting to see some doctor
Because we are no longer waiting for each other
And what we have found can only bloom more,
Like the sun beaming on a seed with its nurturing,
We draw strength
Which will sustain us through whatever,
For our love is as strong as it is tender,
So we have no fear for it will grow
And grow on through the years.

Seán Caomhánach

Poem 45 – THE ONLY MISTAKE

That was the only mistake I think I made Daniela
Always careful with my words
Always only talk of just today we live today
And it was around mid-July
And I'd been on the phone to Kevin
And he was on about Patrick Swayze
And you'd developed a great interest in Patrick Swayze
And following his progress And his health
Because he'd the same pancreatic cancer as you
And he'd been diagnosed with it at around the same time as you
And Kevin was telling me that
He'd seen a photograph of Patrick Swayze eating a big burger
And he was after stacking back on the weight
I sort of doubted the photograph
But I said to you after what Kevin had said about Patrick Swayze
And the photograph of him eating a big burger
And after stacking back on the weight
And I can't remember exactly what you said
But I could see you getting hopeful
And then I made the mistake of saying jokingly
"Yea but the difference between you And him is that he's a multi-
billionaire"
And I'd said it And you'd heard it
And I could see your head drop
And I couldn't take it back
And I could see your hope drop
But I'd said it without thinking
And I knew I'd made a mistake
Because I seen your head And your hope drop
Because I could see you getting angry then
That money was going to determine the length of your life
And nothing against Patrick Swayze

But that photograph of him
Eating a big burger And after stacking back on the weight
Was only a false "Mug-shot"
Because a few weeks after you died
I got a text message on the 14th of September from Michael Carroll
And I was sitting on me armchair in York Street And it just read
"Patrick Swayze is dead Money didn't make any difference"
And nothing against Patrick Swayze
But I just wished I could of forwarded you that text message.

13-December-2009 York Street

Poem 46

I don't think we were even going out with each other for six months
When you came out with another one of your famous wild statements
"I want to be buried with you"
At that time I took it as a threat
I remember backing away from you
I knew you meant it
And I used to attribute your famous wild statements to the fact
That you were from the Mediterranean
An evolution of never ending sun
Genetically stoking emotions
That's what uneased me
I knew your passion was so strong
And after we'd joke about it
After my father died And we'd be up in Mount Venus cemetery
At his grave And we'd be joking about it
"We're going in there Which side do you want No I want that spot"
Although this year
You never went to visit his grave once
Because after the news on the 15th of January
There was no more joking about the likes of that
I must of been thinking it also
Because I never asked you about going up to visit his grave
And that last Sunday in Bonola The 9th of August
I was out on the smoking terrace
Thinking about that famous wild statement you'd made to me when
I don't think we were even going out with each other for six months
"I want to be buried with you"
I was thinking about it And we were in Italy
Thousands of miles from Mount Venus cemetery
And I was worried that you might be worried
That maybe this wouldn't happen now
And I wanted to reassure you that it would

And I was trying to think of a speech
We never really talked about death
That would of been defeatist
So we never talked beyond life
And I was trying to think of some tactful delicate way of saying
"I want to be buried with you"
That the one surety I had in me life was that
I was going to be buried with you
And I was rehearsing me speech
I did a good rehearsal on the smoking terrace
Held it together And went down to your room And eventually
Carefully I got around to it
Sitting up on your bed And I said
"Remember years ago Daniela when you said to me "I want to be
buried with you" Now Daniela I'm not talking about you I'm talking
about me Only hypothetically speaking nothing got to do with you
It's me I don't care where I'm buried once I'm buried with you It
doesn't matter where once we're buried together"
I was way too long-winded
But I thought I was doing real well And tactful with me speech
Holding it together And you said something like
"Ah we were only joking then"
No you weren't joking then
And I wasn't joking now
And then I just started crying
Couldn't help it Couldn't stop it It wasn't in the script
Sitting on your bed
I just started crying And then you said to me
Sort of laughing
"Stop crying you fuckin sap"
I couldn't believe that you'd said that to me at that moment
Yea I'd said it to you hundreds of times
But at that moment it wasn't appropriate
But yea I did stop crying alright

From the fuckin shock of it
And just looking at your smiling face
Through my watery eyes
You got me fuckin lovely
And I knew you meant it when you said
"I want to be buried with you"
And you knew I meant it when I said
"I want to be buried with you"
Because the one surety I have in life is that
Me And you Daniela will be buried together.

14-December-2009 York Street

3rd OF JULY 2004

This is the best part of the day
When night falls and I lie in bed with you
And all the troubles and struggles of this world
Are kept away
Safe and warm under the sky of blankets
Two stars beneath in one bundle
Safe and snuggled in each others arms
Away from all the stress and harms
So let us sleep and dream of these things
That are true
And this is the best part of the day
When night falls and I lie in bed with you.

28-June-04 5 MacDonagh House Golden Lane Dublin 8

Poem 47

I think it was the last Sunday morning or it could of been the last Saturday
And I wasn't sure back then
If you knew for sure what was happening
I'm sure now that you did when
Sitting up on your bed you said
"Have the doctors said anything to you"
(Fuckin right they had)
But I said
"No why have they said anything to you"
Turning defence into attack
And you said "No" And I said
"Well then what are on about so"
That shut you up
And I legged it out to the smoking terrace
Before you'd a chance to think or retaliate
Hit And run before you'd a chance to ask me anymore questions
Feeling sort of pleased with meself for having outsmarted you
And how I'd got the better of you with me answer
But the next day
Sitting on me armchair beside your bed
And you asked me more or less the same question again
"Did the doctors tell you anything"
And I just said "No"
Evasively And obviously not so convincingly because you said
"Ah I can see it in your eyes I'm more foxy than you"
I knew you'd caught me out
And I said nothing but just fixed my eyes on that spot on the floor
Underneath the top-end of your bed
And I was just thinking when you said that word "Foxy"
I've never heard you say that word before
Never And I was wondering where you'd got it from but yeah
You'd done your intelligence-gathering on me alright

So when you said
"I can see it in your eyes"
I said nothing because I couldn't
But after I knew when you said that to me
What I should of said back in reply to you was
"About what"
Bounced your question right back at you
And let you answer it
But sure I wasn't thinking straight
And I wasn't sure then that you knew what I knew
Now I'm sure
You knew that I knew
But I didn't want you to know that I knew
Because I didn't want to know what I knew
But sure you already had to know it
And now I know you were only trying to find out
If I knew
And I fuckin knew alright
Even if I didn't want to know
But I didn't want you to know
What you already had to know
So I just said "No"
Jaysus we turned into terrible liars those last few days
But still at the beautiful head game
Right up to the end
But what else could I say
Because say if I had of said "Yes Fuckin right they have"
Well then there would of been nothing more to say
We would of had nothing more to say to each other
And having nothing more to say to each other
Wasn't a conversation I was ever going to have with you
Although I did have that conversation with you
After I was told that you were dead they closed the door
And I was there for about nearly an hour

Roaring up at you into the ceiling
I knew you could hear me
Because I knew your spirit of Chief Crazy Woman was still in the room
And I was Chief Crazy Man *Dead Can Dance* around the floor
Roaring up at you into the ceiling
Because I could say it then what I knew
Because what I knew had happened
But not before
So I just said "No"
Because I was
Never
Never
Never
Going to say good-bye to you
And now I know that you were only trying to find out if I knew
That you were fucked
And I knew my eyes had betrayed me
(Very clever Very clever My clever little Italian woman)
So I sat there haunched over on me armchair saying nothing
And hid my eyes under that spot on the floor
Underneath the top end of your bed
Where you couldn't see them
And I was just thinking 'Foxy'
'Where did you get that word from "Foxy" Never heard you saying
that word before "Foxy"
And it was over a month later
Around the end of September
And I was out walking one evening along Via Monfalcone
And I wasn't even thinking about it
When it just came to me
'Hendrix Jimi Hendrix *Foxy Lady* That's where you got it from'

And I was sort of pleased with meself
That I'd cracked your code at last
So yea Daniela "More foxy than me"
But I know more about Hendrix than you
Possibly.

15-December-2009 York Street

Poem 48 – THE KKK TOOK MY BABY AWAY

I was sitting in me armchair beside your bed in the hospice
That last Monday night going into Tuesday morning
It must of been around 1 or 2 a.m.
And I was sort of dozing in me armchair
When I heard the words "La puntura"
I knew what those words meant "The injection"
And I knew what that meant
Because I knew the time had come
When they were going to knock you out
You were gonna be sedated
Just like Joey Ramone wanted
Because you'd been agitated a bit that day
Flailing your arms around
Waving And reaching out with them
I knew what that meant
Because I'd seen me father
Flailing his arms around
Waving And reaching out with them
Shortly before he died
So I knew what that meant
He was calling out "Mamma"
Which sort of made me laugh
Because I'd never heard him say that word before
Because she had died nearly 70 years before
And there was this 86 year old dying man
Calling out to his "Mamma"
So that's what he must of called her so IO SO
HE MUST OF SEEN HER FACE AGAIN
So io ho saputo that they were going to send you off
Sleeping into the afterlife
So I got up off me armchair
And stood beside your bed

You were sleeping
And two nurses came into the room
And I was looking at the nurse
Who was banging the "Ketamine" into you
To launch you on your journey
And I was thinking of taking a step forward to hold your hand
As he did it
But instead I found meself taking a step backwards from your bed
As he did it
And I watched him
I don't know why
I haven't psychoanalysed that yet
But there was this dim sallow light in the room
And he had this goaty beard on him
And a sort of Celtic crochet band tattoo on his upper left arm
That just threaded out from under his uniform t-shirt
And I was looking at his goaty beard
In that dim sallow light thinking
'He looks like the devil'
And it was strange
Because I used to pass him several times every night
At the nurses station on me way to And from the smoking terrace
And he used never acknowledge me
Never said "Ciao"
And I knew when I used to pass him at the nurses station
That he was deliberately avoiding any eye or social contact with me
He'd always bury his eyes in his computer screen
Because he must of known that he was a "Humane killer"
Maybe he thought I might hold a grudge against him
So he left his emotions at home
But I was grateful to him
He was doing Joey Ramone's work for you
Fulfilling his wishes
And I would of liked to have told him that

To have thanked him for that
That I understood
But every time I went near him
He'd hide his head away or bury his eyes in his computer screen
And I didn't understand this
Because all the doctors And nurses knew me there
Especially after the row on the smoking terrace
They all knew me
I became like a veteran in that hospice
Six days And Six nights
Not bad for a hospice
I must of been one of the longest serving visitors they ever had there
Sure I was even in the staff kitchen a couple of times
Talking shite And making meself at home
Because at the end
They all knew me by me first name
It was all "Ciao Seán" with all of them
And they even pronounced it right
The most of them didn't even know your name
But they all knew mine
And that's why I didn't understand it with him
It was his job being a "Humane killer"
Maybe that's why he just wanted to be left alone detached
And after he banged the "Knock-out" drug into you
I asked the other nurse that was with him
She spoke a good English so up the corridor after
I asked her if you'd wake up again
And she said you might for a while in the morning
And I said "I doubt it"
But the next morning you did for a while
"Buon giorno"
You wanted to go to the toilet
The nurses had asked me to monitor your bladder movements
And I'd told them that there was nothing happening

And I lifted you up out of your bed
"Uno due tre su" And
Into My Arms
There was such a strong stench of death off you I remember
I wonder did you smell it
And I brought you out to the toilet
And I remember pointing to one of the nurses behind your back
At the blood on your sheet
And I sat you down on the toilet bowl
And nothing only that green stuff in the front of your knickers
I did well to make a joke about it
I was all bravado And hyper cheerfulness
And you sat there for a while but nothing happened
And then I lifted you up
For the last time
"Uno due tre su" And
Into My Arms
For the last time
And you snuggled into me shoulder
And I brought you back to the bed
For the last time
I wonder did you smell it
For you seemed lucid in your mind
And we were talking conversationally
I wonder did you know
Facing what was facing you
You had to know
But you didn't show Tutte palle *Niente Paura*
And I asked you if you wanted to wheel out for a smoke
You'd smoked one the previous morning
But you said "No"
And I knew it was real bad when you didn't want a cigarette
So I helped you back into your bed
And that was that

And there was a couple of nurses running around
Your room doing their jobs
So I just got out of their way
And went out to the smoking terrace for a few cigarettes
Told them the story
And when I came back
You were asleep again
And I knew you wouldn't be waking up again
And I was trying to think of what you'd last said to me
And the nurses were fitting you with the piss-bag
And cleaning your intimate parts
Doing their best for you
To make you comfortable under the circumstances
But sure I didn't really understand what was going on
But I wanted to stay with you
But I shouldn't of been there
Because it was like they were preparing your corpse
And I sat there for about three or four minutes
And then silently tippy-toed out the opening then closing door
Not one squeak did that door make
I went out for a walk I think
And when I came back you were on your own sleeping
And you weren't waking up again
All cleaned all powdered up again
But they'd left your nightdress pulled up around your waist
And then it was a matter of
just Waiting
And I was standing at the end of your bed
Looking at your legs wide open like you were about to give birth
Your eyes were closed
But the garden eye was wide open to me
Garofani Rossi Gigli Rossi Rose Rosa Fucsie Felici Fantasie di Fiori
And through the glass there was
A sun-tongue opening petal lips

So I took off me sandals
And got into your bed with intent And pulled the sheet up over us
I know what I was planning on doing but I couldn't do it
So instead I just held your sleepy head *Into My Arms* for a while
Wake up you sleepy head
No nurses came in
But I couldn't do it
And if don't meet you no more in this world I'll fuck you *in the next one*
won't *be late* won't *be late*
So instead I just held your sleepy head *Into My Arms* for a while
That dark Tuesday night before The 4th of August in Via Mazzini
And I was sitting on your couch
And you stood up from my armchair
And we were getting ready to go to bed And you said
"Do you want to fuck Seán"
And I said
"You're too weak I'd only fuckin kill you"
You were
I should of
The 15th of January on our way back from St. Vincent's
Downstairs on the number 7 bus after more bad news
Bad news comes in busloads And leaning on me left shoulder
You said
"I want to stay with you"
Like a little girl
And you said
"I thought I'd have ten more years with you but now I'll settle for five"
And I said "Yea we can do a lot of things in five years"
It was 7 months after the number 7 bus
That was the dark night that never ended
The night of the blood in the vomit basin
"Too light coloured"
I still had hope
Hope is bullshit

But I fuckin knew alright
You were going to bed And I was going to bed
You were getting up And I was getting up
"Come on to bed Daniela"
You were deliriously out of your head
I put me arms around you where you were sitting at the table
And tried to lift you into the bedroom
I didn't know what to do
So I just stayed there with me arms around you
just Waiting for the light of morning
You were deliriously out of your head And so was I
"Come on to bed Daniela"
That dark Tuesday night before
When even blood seemed the colour of light
"Do you want to fuck Seán"
I should of said "Si"
So instead I just held your sleepy head *Into My Arms* for a while
Wake up and make love with me Wake up and make love
And then it was a matter of
just Waiting
At least the following week the nights were shorter in the hospice
Started to get bright around 6am
And then around 9am
I said into your ear that last morning
I knew you could hear me
Because I knew the hearing was the last to go
Before the breath that is so I said
Like I said every morning
"Buon giorno Daniela" And kissed you
And then I watched your mouth move And silently mime
"Buon giorno"
So now I know that's the last words you said to me Daniela
"Buon giorno"
Like the first words I still say to you every morning.

16-December-2009 York Street

Poem 49

I can see the snow on the Dublin Mountains
Today from the balcony
First time in the new gaff
I thought of you
And how you'd of been impressed with that
I thought of you
And how we could of looked at the snow on the Dublin Mountains
together
Today from the balcony
First time in the new gaff
And I'd of probably patriotically stated
About how the snow on the Dublin Mountains
Was far more impressive
Than any snow I'd ever seen on your Italian Alps
Certainly had great potential there for a row about
How my Irish snow on my Irish mountain
Was far more impressive
Than your Italian snow on your Italian Alps
I'd say that we wouldn't of been talking to each other
For at least a week after that one.

18-December-2009 York Street

I DIDN'T KNOW YOU WROTE THE POETRY AS WELL DANIELA BUT I KNOW WHAT YOU MEAN

The hour of departure has arrived,
And we go our separate ways,
I do die,
And you to live.
Which of these two is better only God knows.

Daniela Picerni – Circa 2009

Poem 50

That last Wednesday morning the 12th of August
I went over to that church just opposite the hospice
S.S. Martiri Anaunies on Via Ugo Ojetti
To say my prayer Light a candle for you like I did every morning
I'd went over to it also that last Tuesday morning
The day before
To say my prayer Light a candle for you like I did every morning
For a year And a half in
Whitefriar Notre Dame Arluno Rozzano Bonola Dappertutto
But on that last Tuesday morning
The day before
I'd changed my prayer but then changed it back again because
"I'm not giving up either"
But on that last Wednesday morning
I'd given up
I knew the miracle wasn't going to happen
And I had really believed in the miracle
Because it was easier to believe in the miracle
Than what it was to believe in the alternative
Because I thought I had friends with influence
San Antonio San Pellegrino San Francesco San Pio
And I'd always drop a euro in the box for the candle
To intercede so as to hear my prayer
Not that I felt I needed to
Because they were all Italians
You were one of their own
All Italians All Your People
I thought that they could of been a bit more nationalistic about things
But on that last Wednesday morning
I'd given up
And I lit my candle
But I changed my prayer

And I wasn't praying to any Italians anymore
Because I should of prayed all along to some Irish Saint like
Saint Patrick Good quality Good quality
Because I was praying to My Own People now
My Father And My Granny
My Granny who I'd prayed to
To bring you into my life in the first place
So I prayed to them My Own People
To welcome you And to look after you
Show you the way around
And I lit my candle as usual
But just to show the Italians I said to
San Antonio San Pellegrino San Francesco San Pio
Where normally I just put one euro in the box for the candle
That morning I put in two euro
Just to show the Italians
And looking right up at the statues face I said out loud
"No hard feelings"
And dropped the two euro in the box
I could of said a lot more
But I held meself back
Because I swore I wouldn't become bitter
And after a walk to *Regina Di Pace*
I walked back to the hospice
Sure that My Father And My Granny would welcome you
just Sitting down beside your bed
just Sitting guard uselessly
just Waiting for the thief to take you.

6-January-2010 York Street

Poem 51

There around last September
And I was upstairs in Paolo Colombo's gaff on Via Mazzini
And Luca Magni And Gianluca Bianchi were there also
And I was after cooking the "Chilli con carne"
They all think in Arluno that chilli con carne
Is a traditional Irish dish
And we were talking And drinking afterwards
And I must of been whinging on about things
Because Gianluca said something
I didn't catch it all
And I knew Gianluca had lost both his parents when he was young
And I knew he had no brothers or sisters
And I knew he had to get used to losing loved ones
And being on his own from a young age
So my situation maybe seemed a bit usual to him
And we were all a bit drunk
And I'm saying about how everyone loses someone you love
If you live long enough
And I'm trying not to make a big deal about it
Because it happens all the time
And all the time people get on with it
And all the time worse shit is happening to more people
And I'm not the first
And I won't be the last
But all's I was trying to say was
That it was the first time it had happened to me
So yea
I am the first
So I'll whinge all I fuckin well like about it.

6-January-2010 York Street

Poem 52

You said to me one day
Towards the end of July in Via Mazzini
We were talking about something else
And you said
"You're naïve Seán"
But not in a bad or malicious way
But it bothered me a bit
But I didn't get touchy about it
How could I with you in your condition
So I said nothing
But under normal circumstances
I would of reacted with a row
'What do mean I'm naïve You mean I'm a fuckin eejit Is that what
you're saying A fool Is that what you mean because that's what that
polite word "naïve" means'
Although you did say to me once
Years ago you said
"Any other woman would have kick you up the arse"
And I said
"Nobody kicks me up the arse woman or man And gets away with it
And you won't either"
True
You never did either
You did kick me in the chest And the stomach alright
But never up the arse
Maybe that's what you meant by "Naïve"
And you could be a little bit naïve yourself on occasions
Only for me putting you wide
But say even if I can be on occasions

A little bit naïve Daniela
I knew I could always shelter
My thoughts And words on the snug of your tongue
And they would be safely left unsaid.

30-January-2010 York Street

**Poem 53 – THERE IS A LIGHT THAT NEVER GOES OUT
5-SEPTEMBER-1997 – THE INTERNATIONAL BAR**

Take me out tonight
Because I want to see people
And I want to see life

I'd been out the night before
But I hadn't been out in over three weeks before that so
I knew I'd be on a bender
I knew me form
Used to hit it for about a week every month
Go mad for a few days
Me periods I used to call them
And I'd been out the night before
Did a comedy gig in the International
And one in the Norseman on the same Thursday night
Good going for me to do two in one night
Because normally for me it was about two or three every two or
three months
And I'd been up late that Thursday night
And got up early enough the next day
And I was still sort of drunk so
I decided to head down to the International
For a bit of "Topping up" for the "Goo"
And rang Kevin in his work on me way down
From them public phones that used be beside the Gaiety
To meet him there for lunch

23-December-09

He must of arrived in about 1pm
And we sat down in the corner inside the door
And he ordered tea with a ham 'n cheese sandwich

And I must of been on about me second or third pint
And he's sniffing at his sandwich the way he does
And speculating that the sandwich is not the best
That there's a bit of smell off it
That the ham was gone off
And I didn't want to be making a big deal about it
Sure so were the pints but that wasn't stopping me getting them
down into me
But he's wary about eating the sandwich
And it's after been paid for And all
So after a while of him going on about it
I brought it back up again to Alan Martin the barman
And told him the sandwich seemed a bit gone off
And would he mind changing it
And Alan speculated that the sandwich wasn't a bit gone off at all
I wasn't sure either way
But you know Kevin's sensitive sense of smell
So he exchanged it anyway
And Kevin still reckoned that the second sandwich was also a bit gone off
For fucksake but he ate that one anyway
And we were just there talking
Can't remember about what
But I presume it was either family sport or politics
And then he had to go back to work about 2pm
And I'm sitting there in the corner inside the door
On them seats down the end near the toilets
On me own surveying around the bar
Looking to see who I could antagonise
Or how I was going to entertain meself for the afternoon
And I remember you coming in up the far door about 2pm
But I didn't pay much attention to you
Remember you crossing the floor
Towards the taps
But I didn't scrutinise you

Didn't really look at you
Just remember you crossing my line of vision
You weren't a target
And you walked to the centre of the bar
Where the taps are
And it was then you really caught my attention
Because you ordered a plain cheese sandwich
And a glass of Guinness
And I was up out of me corner
And I was standing at the bar taps beside you waiting for me pint
And I was giving out fuck about the sandwiches
Nothing got to do with you
I was only trying to wind Alan up
Antagonise him
And I retreated back to me corner with me pint
And you sat down just up from me with your plain cheese sandwich
And your glass of Guinness
And I remember raising my voice up to you
"I wouldn't eat that if I were you"
But I wasn't interested in you
I was only interested in winding Alan up
You were just the window through which I saw my opportunity
Because that was going to be my entertainment for the afternoon
I'd of been bored sitting there on me own
So my entertainment was going to be
Antagonising Slagging   Alan
And his stale substandard more than a bit gone off sandwiches
And you became the means of how I was going to achieve this
And it was from then that I started addressing you directly
Not Alan
But saying it real loud so as he had to hear me
The whole bar could hear my denunciation
Of the sandwich you were eating
Especially that oul fella who sat down in the middle of us

As I was in the middle of my sandwich denunciation
And I wasn't trying to chat you up
I was just trying to wind you up
About the fatal sandwich you were eating
But you were eating it
And I was telling you
Not to worry
I'll call an ambulance for you
Because that's the caring sort I am
And did you know that food poisoning can kill you
But not to worry I'll call an ambulance for you
I'm considerate like that
And I'm really getting inspired with my tirade
The shite I was coming out with
Never realised I could condemn a sandwich so much
Must of railed against it constantly non-stop for twenty minutes or
half an hour
And I'm raising my voice to you
And I remember you looking at me And laughing
And smiling at me
With an orange chiffon scarf around your neck
And somewhere I must of been thinking
'Yeah you're alright'
And asking you how you feel after that last bite
Do you notice anything yet
Are you still alright
Or will I call an ambulance for you now
And you're laughing
And Alan is fuckin bullin behind the counter
He wasn't seeing the funny side
And maybe some of the other customers weren't either
Having their peace disturbed
But sure you were laughing
You understood

You got it
And sure I was enjoying meself
Fuckin relentlessly on a roll
And Alan comes down to me
After enduring a lot
But sure I wasn't even talking to him I was talking to you
None of his earwigging business
And leaning over me
Angry And Apologetically at the same time he said
"If you keep this up Seán I'm going to have to bar you"
And going on about how other customers might believe me
(It wasn't the first time I'd done that as some tourists had believed me
about the soup before And then walked out after I condemned it)
About the stale substandard sandwiches
And I was pondering my predicament then between us
When that oul fella who had sat down in the middle of us
When I was in the middle of my sandwich denunciation
The innocent bystander
Stood up from his seat
And walked over towards the side of the bar at the ladies toilet
Turned around then And said as he finished his pint of Smithwicks
Never saw him before Never saw him again
Don't think he was a local
He probably never went back there again
He probably didn't fancy the food poisoned sandwiches
And he said to us
"Either you move up there or you move down there"
And I was real settled in me corner so I said
"Well I'm not moving"
But before I had a chance to elaborate on me sentence
You had already stood up to make your way down
And I was sort of standing up as well And I said
"Well I don't mind moving up either All the one to me"
And before I'd finished that sentence

You were already standing beside me
So we sat down in the corner
And I wasn't trying to chat you up
I was just trying to wind you up

31-December-09

…………………………………

12-February-2010

And I didn't even offer to buy you a drink
For about me next two pints
Just in case you thought I was
And besides sure you were only drinking a glasheen
Which for me is only a waste anyway
And I suppose the first thing I must of established
The usual unoriginal question about origin
Is that you were an Italian
And the first subjects you always discuss with someone
When you're first just introduced to each other
When you're first just getting to know each other
First rule is
Always discuss politics And religion
After I asked where you were from
Must of asked you your name before that
Italy Milano
So straight away I started rearing up about Berlusconi
And what a fascist bastard he is
And what sort of idiots could elect him
I was hoping you were a Berlusconi supporter
But by jaysus you gave it back to me
And how much you hated Berlusconi
And you're giving out fuck about Italian politics

And that fascist bastard Berlusconi
And how you were for the Communist party
Fausto Bertinotti Antonio Gramsci Fidel Castro Che Guevara
(Remember that time a few years ago
And I was sitting on me armchair
And you were sitting on your couch
And we were watching the telly
And something came on the telly about an award
For the greatest Irish-American of all time
And I said
"The greatest Irish-American of all time is Che Guevara"
Séamus Guevara Ó Loinsoigh
And I had to explain it to you
But you were laughing
But you were impressed so much so that
I think you only put half a plate of spaghetti in front of me afterwards
You were that impressed)
And how you were for the Communist Party
Fausto Bertinotti Antonio Gramsci Fidel Castro Che Guevara
And how you'd stood in local elections for them
Getting somewhere in between 11 And 13 votes I think
And you were pissed off that you'd got that many votes
Because you'd canvassed people not to vote for you
So you reckoned that there was in between 11 And 13 people
In Arluno who didn't like you
And I couldn't get a word in with all your giving out
With all the laughing we were doing at that arsehole
So there was no point pursuing that one
Because I didn't have the expertise of knowledge on him
Like you did
And I'm trying to change the subject
Return to more familiar territory
An argument I can win
Because you're getting wound up alright

But not getting wound up the way I'd intended
So I'm on about books And literature then
"Yea I read a book by an Italian once Alberto Moravio The Conformist
Wasn't great as a matter of fact it was boring"
I was hoping you were a fan of Moravio
That you really liked him
But you weren't interested in him at all
Instead you were interested in Stefano Benni
And started going on about Stefano Benni
Never heard of him
A great writer you were saying
A great Italian writer was what you meant
And saying he was very similar to Flann Ó Brien
Yea I'd read a bit of Flann Ó Brien in me days
But fuck it you'd read more
And you knew more about Flann Ó Brien than I did
So I moved on about the RA then
And about the war in the occupied six-counties
And about the war of anti-imperialist resistance was the only thing
that made me feel
Proud to be Irish
Is that an orange sash you're wearing
At least there's some excuse for them
And about how there's always only been about
Five percent of the people in this country
With the balls of resistance
To stand up to the
Five percent who run And control
Everything Everywhere
And the other ninety percent in between the stools the stools the stools
And it doesn't matter who you vote for because that
Five percent at the top will always run And control
Everything Everywhere
Because they don't give a fuck who you vote for

The will of the people
The will of the five percent at the top
And I'm misquoting Connolly
And I'm misquoting Pearse
And praising the Ten Hunger-Strikers
With the balls of resistance
Against the running dog colonialist treacherous rats imperialist pigs
Wading knee deep in Irish blood
And I like animals
And the conversation is going from the International
All around the international world
Internazionale Forza Inter Roberto Baggio
A bit of order
And banging down me pint glass on the table
After me speech
And of course
You knew all about that as well
It must of ignited in all that anger
It must of ignited in all that laughter
But you lose the strength
You lose the will
You lose the faith
You lose the fight
Except to fight with meself
The enemy within returns again
End up not giving a fuck
Become one of the zero percent
"I've lost my anger This disease has taken away my anger"
You'd a curious mind anyway
Saying to me that I was
"Curious as a snake"
And you knew all about Irish culture
And all about Irish music
And going back as far as The Celts

I remember we were on about Alan Stivell as well
Think I saw him once up in The National Boxing Stadium about 1976
Think you saw him more than once though
Jaysus can a man not spoof around here anymore
And telling me the place you were from in Italy
Had a Celtic name
Arluno Altar of the Moon
The Celts named it
So I knew I was going nowhere with that either
So I started giving out fuck
No it was you that started giving out fuck first
About the big deal in this country about
Some English princess that was killed in a car crash in Paris
And I remember you giving out fuck more than me And you said
"What that got to do with this country"
You out-extremed me there
And I was sorry that I hadn't thought of saying that first
And I'm going out of me way to agree with you
That wasn't the plan because
I wasn't trying to chat you up
I was just trying to wind you up
But I wasn't having much success
And after a while I was thinking
'Yea you're deffo alright'
And I said
"Let me get you a drink but not a glass because they're a rip-off"
And explaining to you the price structure of mark-ups
So I got you a pint the next drink
No sandwich
And then you said about
How you'd just come into town on your day off
From the chipper in Howth to buy a ticket for
Shane McGowan And The Popes
And I was laughing thinking

'You come into town on your day off to buy a ticket for Shane
McGowan And you
meet me meet me already nearly pissed drunk at 2 o clock in the day'
Now that's Poetry
And you're showing me your ticket
Just one ticket
And there was me thinking that I was the only one
Who ever went to events on me own
And I like Shane McGowan
And we're talking about The Doors
And we're talking about The Smiths
And we're talking about good old Joe Strummer And his "Smash
H-Block" t-shirt
And John Lennon And his "Red mole for the IRA against British
imperialism" poster
Seán Ó Leannáin
No Vietcong ever called him a "Paddy"
And we can't agree more
Tell me again about how once
You threw the flowers up at Morrissey at a gig in Milan
And Morrissey picked them up
And how you'd a record shop in Arluno for six years
And it must of been about 5 minutes to 5
Or 5 minutes to 6
(No I asked Alan after And he said the shift changed at 5.30 but sure
he was sobber so how would he know)
When I seen Simon McEvoy the barman
Arriving in up at the far door with his bicycle for his shift
I used to know all the barmen's shifts there
I had their rosters in me head
And I saw him arriving in up at the far door with his bicycle for his shift
And I panicked a bit
I knew I had to get you offside out of there
Because if he saw me talking with a woman

I knew he'd only be asking me afterwards about you
How I got on And that
And then I'd only have to bullshit him a bit about how I was only
talking to you
'An Italian A tourist I think Just talking Wasn't interested'
So I knew I had to get you offside out of there
Before he seen me with you
Pressure on to proposition
So I said about
How there was paintings on the walls up in Grogan's
Just up the street a bit
And about how very interesting they are
Bullshitting you about how cultured I was
And interested in art
Because I knew that if you agreed to leave the International with me
And come up to Grogan's with me
You were interested
You were "In the bag" "Nel pugno"
And you're bullshitting me about how interested you would be
In seeing those paintings on the walls up in Grogan's
And I was under pressure of time before Simon seeing us together
(But as it turned out we weren't really bullshitting all that much
Because we went to loads of galleries And art exhibitions
everywhere after)
And as we walked from the International bar
Simon didn't see us together
By the time he got himself organised behind the bar
We were walking up South William Street
Singing The Smiths
And we sat down on them seats
Up in the bar corner beside the toilet in Grogan's
And we were singing a duet
Do you know you can get barred for singing here
I was barred the first time I was ever in it

Not for singing though just for being drunk
But I got back in again
And we were singing a duet
On them seats
Up in the bar corner beside the toilet in Grogan's
And I must of been well drunk by this stage
And we're talking And laughing And talking And laughing
And singing with our mouths open
And I just sort of leaned Or lunged at you
And kissed you in that corner
And for fuck sake
You kissed me back
"Nel pugno alright"
And we were singing a duet
Except I kept singing the words wrong to you
There ain't nobody that can sing like me
And you were singing the words right
And if a double-decker bus
Crashes into us
To die by your side
Is such a heavenly way to die
Remember Glendalough
And that conversation we had
On the 27th of September 1997
(I found the photographs of that day in the cupboard with the date
on the back of them
I knew you'd keep And file And date them my organised woman)
And we took the St. Kevin's bus from "The Green"
And I brought a flask of tea
And made up tinned salmon sandwiches with brown bread
You only ate a bit of the sandwiches
But I liked them anyway
And we had our picnic beside the lake
And I picked you a heart shaped pebble

And gave it to you
I found it in the pink box in the cupboard when I got back in November
Wrapped in tinfoil
I know that's the one you fuckin sap
I knew you'd keep it
Like all the others
At a lake or the sea
I'd pick you a heart shaped pebble
Like a fuckin sap
But I didn't have the balls to say it to you
We would of had to talk about death
Well then there would of been nothing more to say
We would of had nothing more to say to each other
And having nothing more to say to each other
Wasn't a conversation I was ever going to have with you
But in Glendalough as we were walking around after the picnic
Beside the lake And I said
"We'll go together"
We said we'd go together
If anything was to happen to either of us
We were laughing when we were saying it in Glendalough
We never mentioned it again though
Just that day
And we were laughing
The glen of the two lakes
The one would of done us
The deepest
Together
Were we joking or were we serious
Maybe I was just sounding you out
Just seeing how you'd respond
Up the ante Up the ante
Hit you with the heavy shit
And see how you'd react

Sure we were only together a couple of weeks
Hardly knew each other but knew that
You were it And I was it
And that was that
And I was laughing when I said it
But I wasn't joking
Just maybe testing to see if you'd go all the way with me
It didn't seem strange to you at all
You understood
And you said you'd go all the way into the lake with me
We'd go together
You weren't joking
You were serious
I knew you meant it
That was the response I wanted as I was laughing
Just to see how far you'd go with me
All the way
Because that response meant more than "I do"
Up the ante Up the ante
You seen me but you didn't raise me
Not that time anyway
But we never mentioned it again
But I remember it
Say I had of said it to you
You would of fought me
But I knew you needed me alive
For a little while longer anyway
But we said it twelve years ago
Jokers in the pact
We'll go together in Glendalough
A nice day A great day
But sure we even argued after about what sort of a day it was
The glen of the one lake for us
But it was a great day

All so laughing And peaceful And faraway now
But I did think about it the last year
Just briefly Not deeply
But we were youngish back then
I had to stay alive for you or was it for me
What's balls
They're what you had
Mi dai le tue palle Daniela
You were dying anyway
Oh what difference does it make
None at all
Twelve years ago in Glendalough is a faraway time ago
And a lot of lakes And heart shaped pebbles in between
Como Garda Maggiore
We did all those lakes together
But I remember Glendalough more
When we could talk about death And laugh
When we could talk about death And a lake
We were supposed to go together
Thinking of a *double-decker bus And*
But I didn't mention it
I couldn't mention death
Say I had of mentioned it
You would of fought me anyway
You said to me a few times Sort of giving out
"You fight windmills"
But I didn't fight the windmills
You're the one who fought the windmill
I fight my own corner That's all
But it was a lot easier to fight when you were in my corner
You were always watching my back
I could trust you
That's trust
I watched the smile dying in the jaws of your face

It was too much for you
But it was too much for me as well
I remember that expression on your face in Bonola
I'd be watching you when I thought you weren't watching
Sitting up on your bed
I've been thinking about that
Thinking what you must of been thinking
Thinking about how you reconciled yourself to the
Inevitable Unstoppable
And I know what you were thinking
No need to ask
How you accepted death was by thinking
That you had twelve great years together with me
That's how you accepted Handled it
And that makes me feel ashamed
Jaysus you were so easy to please
You didn't ask for much
And you got cancer Fuckin cancer
Deliver me my vengeance for you Against who The Windmills
Profondo nel mio cuore sono un terrone
And you never complained
Was I the highlight of your life Daniela
Because that makes me feel ashamed
But when my time comes
I will do the same as you
And I will think
I had twelve great years together with you
The highlight of my life
And I won't feel ashamed
(Because I don't remember before you so well
And there's nothing worth remembering after you)
You'd enough to be thinking of with your own dying
Without thinking of mine as well
But I didn't have the balls to say it to you

We would of had to talk about death
I have them now
Because I'm not afraid of it now
You set the precedent
You did all the hard work as usual
"I know you" too
The hour of departure has arrived,
And we go our separate ways,
I do die,
And you to live.
I found that in the back of your 2008 "Smemoranda" diary
When I got back in November
Don't know when you wrote it so
I do this instead
Because it can't be any worse
What have I become my sweetest friend
You knew I'd find it because I'm
"Curious as a snake"
I do die,
And you to live.
Which of these two is better only God knows.
(No it's Socrates after he was condemned to death
Mick Doyle copped it
You left me Socrates
Now I know why you had no fear
You left me Socrates)
I do this instead Daniela
This is better *only God knows*
Because it can't be any worse
Because I want to tell the people the sort of Daniela you were
And not just "Half of Dublin" either
This is how I hold onto you
My left hand in your right hand
Very clever Very clever

Or remember that time about seven or eight years ago
When you bought me the cap for me birthday
In Coyle's hat and cap outfitters on Aungier Street
And as soon as we entered Coyle's door
The old man Coyle there said to me
From a good six feet away
Straight away just on first sight without any measure
"You've a double crown"
And that made sense
Because I could never find a cap to fit me
And you said "What's a double crown"
And I was sort of winding you up a bit
And I said "A double crown That means I've two brains"
And for a good while after that statement
Any time I'd get drunk And make a fuckin eejit out of meself
You had your childish little mantra
"Ah you with your two brains Why you don't even use one of them"
But I suppose I can tell you now Daniela
I didn't really like it when you used to say that to me
But sure what could I say back
You thought I was clever
You said it
But in some things I am In others I'm not
Together we were clever
Just the right balance
If the world had of declared war against us
The world would of lost
You were dying anyway
I wanted not to be here anymore on that last Saturday
Or at least blast meself into oblivion
Maybe they're the same thing
Nobody knows for sure
Know Feel Nothing
Certainly not pain

I hurt myself today to see if I still feel
I focus on the pain
The only thing that's real
I had to stay alive for you
It would of been easier for me to go
I wanted to go
Bang some of that stuff they were injecting into you into me
So that was balls
I'm still fuckin here
And we were youngish back then
When we could talk about death And laugh in Glendalough
Besides you said on the corridor of St. Vincent's on the 8th of June
when you called me
"I won't leave you"
But I don't see you
But you won't leave me
But I can't see you
But you won't leave me
But I don't see you
Except when I close my eyes
I see images of you when I close my eyes
Except when I open my eyes
I see images of you when I open my eyes
I WILL SEE YOUR FACE AGAIN when
I'm flailing my arms around
Waving And reaching out with them so IO SO
I WILL SEE YOUR FACE AGAIN
But you have to help me now
It's your turn
I'm deep inside myself but I'll get out somehow
"I won't leave you"
What have I become my sweetest friend
Yea I must of been really drunk to try that
But sure it worked

I think after that kiss we only had the one more
If we'd one at all
Sang a few more songs though
And I was saying to you about
How I only live up the street
It's near not far
(Too near sometimes)
I only live up the street
Do you want to come back and we can listen to The Smiths
We both understood The Smiths
You threw the flowers up at Morrissey at a gig in Milan
Because we both felt The Smiths
Because we both knew The Smiths
Because we both understood The Smiths
And all these academic arseholes in universities
Shiteing on about the plight of post-modern futility And isolation
But The Smiths are not just about the words
It's about the feeling
You either feel it or you don't
And fuck the analysis
And you either feel it or you don't
And you either know it or you don't
And you either understand it or you don't
Last night I dreamt that somebody loved me
Only an arsehole
Who feels nothing
Who knows nothing
Who understands nothing
Could analyse that
And Morrissey picked them up
Stiofán Pádraig Ó Muirgheasa
Real proud of it you were
Worse than me for repeating yourself
And I think it must of been starting to get dark when we came out

And I was barely able to stand up
And I remembered I was supposed to see Michael Carroll in Toner's
at 9pm
But I sort of forgot about that
And I remember walking up South William Street with you
Drunk as I was I remember it
And I remember we were wrapped around each other
Singing And Laughing
And if a ten-ton truck
Kills the both of us
To die by your side
Well the pleasure-the privilege is mine
Thinking of a *double-decker bus And a ten-ton truck*
And just there at Mercer Street Lower near the corner
I nearly fell over onto the street
But you held me up
Because there is always that strong gale of wind
That blows down Mercer Street Lower we agreed
And I staggered And you walked
Holding me up them four flights of stairs
In the old York Street into the gaff
With the smell of piss on the stairs
And junkies blood on the walls
And the state of me
There isn't a woman in this world
Who would of climbed up them four flights of stairs with me but you
You didn't give it a fuckin damn Tutte palle *Niente Paura*
Niente Paura- No fear-Ligabue
You bought that CD as a present for me at Malpensa Airport in
March 2008
On our way home after the cancer had been confirmed
I used to sing it-*Niente Paura*-No Fear
Especially when I was full of fear
And I put on The Smiths

And sat down on me armchair
And you were dancing around the floor And you said
For me to get up and dance
And I said "I don't fuckin dance"
I didn't either before I met you
Maybe you don't remember all those times I said to you in the hospice
You were sleeping most of the times I said it
All the times I said to you in the hospice
"Nothing will separate us Daniela nobody will separate us nothing will separate us"
"Nothing will separate us nothin nient nessun nobody nessun nient nothin"
My mantra
My song
You were dead And I didn't know it And I was still saying it
"Nothing will separate us"
"La mia bella donna piccola"
I'd never said that to you before
But I didn't fuckin dance
I didn't either
And then I managed to get up off me armchair
And I was up dancing with you
Nothing could separate us
Because you had to hold me up
But I was dancing with you
And we were dancing
And singing our duet
Along to The Smiths
There is a light that never goes out
There is a light that never goes out
There is a light that never goes out

EPILOGUE

12-February-2010 9.15pm

Last night I dreamt that somebody loved me
Because when I woke up the next morning
In that small creaky single bed
I'd got over in Bride Street
Somebody was in me bed
I remember the morning opening me eyes
And seeing And feeling
Somebody was in me bed
I didn't know who you were
I didn't know how you'd got there
I was badly hungover with black-out memory loss first thing
So I just lay still on the flat of me back without moving
Afraid to move in case I might wake you
Wouldn't of known what to say to you
In hindsight I suppose I could of said to you
If you had of awoken by surprise
Hello I love you won't you tell me your name
That would of impressed you
And I was trying to piece together the previous day
Lying still on the flat of me back without moving
Trying to retrace me movements
'Went to the International bar
Met Kevin for lunch
Yea
Then this Italian arrived in
That's who you are
The Italian'
Bits of obliterated conversation slowly regrouping
Then we went to Grogan's
Jaysus And I kissed you in the bar corner beside the toilet in Grogan's

Yea most of it started coming back to me
And just there at Mercer Street Lower near the corner
I nearly fell over onto the street
Just as well there wasn't a *ten-ton truck* passing
Yea that fuckin gale of wind that always blows down Mercer Street
Lower
And I quietly raised my back
Craning my head
To see if I could get a look at you to see who you were
But you were facing the wall with your back to me
And I was terrified of waking you
Until I'd established a few more facts
And I quietly raised my back a second time
Craning my head to take a peep over
To see if I could get a look at you to see who you were
But I remember your hair
Was drawn down the right side of your face
And I was trying to remember your name
Yea things were coming back to me after some hard concentration
But what was your name
Because apparently women can get offended about stuff like that
But how the fuck was I supposed to remember everything
I was pissed drunk all the previous day for fucksake
Not easy to remember when you wake up first thing in the morning
And then I remembered
Yes you're the Italian
And your name is Daniela
Thanks be to jaysus for that
It came to me after about fifteen minutes
Lying still on the flat of me back without moving
With the exception of two peeps over for about fifteen minutes of terror
Dan-yell-ah
Not Danielle because that's French
It's Daniela because you're Italian

At least that was a good start
Established a few facts
I could relax a bit more now
I remembered your name after about fifteen minutes
So I got up for a piss then
Didn't matter if I woke you up now
And I remember seeing your handbag
Lying on the sitting room floor just inside the door
And then standing over it thinking
'Well you're bound to have some I.D. in your handbag
Something with your name on it
Just to be 100 percent sure'
I was thinking of having a root through your handbag
Just to confirm Just to establish your name for certain
But then I was thinking
'What if you wake up
And come out into the sitting room
And catch me rooting through your handbag
Sure then you'd just think that I was a thief
And then if I explained Protesting my innocence
No nothing like that I'm just only trying to establish for certain
What your name is'
Which would of been worse
What a hangover The Stress Me nerves were in bits Potts gone
So I left your handbag Didn't touch it
Because I was sure
Because I'd thought about it Concentrated hard
And then I remembered your name is definitely Daniela
And the next thing I remember
Is being in the bath washing me feet with me trouser ends pulled up
And we were up by this stage
And I was confidently addressing you as "Daniela"
Sure how could I forget a name like that
And the bathroom in the old York Street was very small

And I'm standing in the bath washing me feet with me trouser ends pulled up

And you were standing at the bathroom door with your formal polite English

That must be taught in language schools

That nobody ever speaks like

And you were talking

And I'm explaining to you about how I have sweaty feet

Knowing that there was no possibility of me asking you out

I could say what I felt like with no possibility of me asking you out

I'd given up on that

Best to leave things the way they are now

And I was nearly 37 years old

And planning on being dead by 45

Had it all worked out

I didn't have too much longer to wait

And I would of been too Only for you

Because I always thought you'd outlive me

Your genetics on both sides

They all lived into their 90's

A woman who loved me to mourn me

That would of been a comfort

For me

Now it's a man who loved you to mourn you

No comfort for me

What have I become my sweetest friend

Practically speaking you'd of been better able to handle this than me because

"You're tougher than me You're tougher than me"

I had depended on you not dying before me

And I was explaining about me sweaty feet

Knowing that there was no possibility of me asking you out

I'd already resolved that it was just me féin

Because I knew I could live life on me own

Back then
But back now
These mornings when the sun rises
After about 9pm in the evening
Then sinks under the darkness of my eyelids for the night
When I try to sleep
"I can't sleep Daniela"
What have I become my sweetest friend
That's the way it is now Accept it Get on with it
Before I met you
Not so sure after though without you
The dependency develops
And I have to go back to the way I was before
But before it was normal for me
I didn't know any different
But now the balance is gone
And I've become lop-sided
I can't go back to the way I was before either
There's no where to go
No where to go to
No where to retreat to
And I'm back here on York Street on me own again But
I'm a million miles away I'm a million miles away
Sailing like a drift-wood on a windy day
Never thought you'd die before me so
I refuse to recognise the court
And you were standing at the bathroom door with your formal
polite English
And saying about this Shane McGowan gig in just under two weeks
And I'm explaining about the importance of drying well in between
the toes
And bacteria And all that sort of stuff
It's very important to dry well in between the toes
And you were saying about how you could get a second ticket

And we could go to see Shane McGowan together
And I said
"Yea I like Shane McGowan"
Emphasising him because I knew
I could throw meself at Shane McGowan alright
Séaghan MacGabhann
But I had me benders planned
Me periods I used to call them
And I was on one then
And going down to Strokestown for the Agricultural Show that day
And wouldn't be back 'til Tuesday or Wednesday normally
Depending on the finance of funds
And I wouldn't have the money to be out again for me next bender
For at least another three weeks
Can you imagine me trying to explain that to you
So that's why I said I'd see you in about three weeks
I had me plans
And I wouldn't have the money to be out again
But sure "We'll see"
And you said you could get the ticket anyway
But you see I had established me own survival system
That I knew how its routines worked
And I wouldn't be out again
For at least another three weeks
I had me system Didn't like it being upset
And then we were talking in the sitting room
I was giving out fuck about this And that
And talking about the previous day
I'd remembered the most of the detail by then
And we had both laughed all that day
And you told me a few years later
That you didn't really understand too much of what I was saying that day
Talking too fast Accent Slurring me words
And you spent the whole day laughing

I was nearly getting touchy about that after when you told me that
That you didn't really understand too much of what I was saying
Because if you didn't really understand too much of what I was
saying that day
Well then why did you spend the whole day laughing
What the fuck were you laughing at
I was nearly getting touchy about that after when you told me that
A Joe Pesci job
'You think I'm funny Funny how I amuse you You think I'm a
fuckin clown'
But I decided to leave it And let it go
But you laughed all that day
I know now why you spent the whole day laughing
But at the time I didn't cop it
I should of known
But sure I always read the signs wrong
But sure I was always happy with you
Even in an angry row inside I'd still be happy to have you here
Because you were always more than enough women for me
The only woman I ever wanted
I'm not greedy but I was greedy for you
Slurp slurp
That's why in that first year or two
Your jealousy so fuckin offended me
That's why I got so vindictive
You give it You get it back
You gave it You got it back
Up the ante Up the ante
You kill one of mine And I'll kill ten of yours
You kill ten of mine And I'll kill one hundred of yours
You gave me all
"Everything for my Seán"
You got it back
You're still getting it back

You started it You get it back
Up the ante Up the ante
I could never understand it
I used to think about it
I could never understand what you saw in me
I could never understand your faith in me
I used to think that it would wear off after a year or two
You'd get bored disappointed with me
Because I used to think you couldn't keep this up
I gave you a year or two to let it settle thinking
'You can't keep this up You have to wane'
But you didn't
And after about a year or two I stopped thinking about it
I just accepted it And stopped trying to understand it
Because I couldn't understand it
Because why do I always have to try And understand things
Because there was nothing I could do about it
So I accepted it
That was the way you were
No point thinking about it
So instead I just thought about the way you were
And I knew you were true then
Slurp slurp
Remember I'd be singing that song
I'm a lucky man
Except I kept singing the words wrong to you
I'm a lazy man
There's a lot to be said for a lazy man
I think you preferred my version
Or that other roaring row we had a few years ago
"you love me more"
"no you love me more"
"no you love me more"
"no you love me more"

"no you love me more You're too much I can't match you"
"no you love me more"
Can't remember for how long we didn't speak to each other after that one
But I was always happy with you
I know you were always happy with me
More Italian maybe
Wasn't my way
I express meself a different way
Sometimes it's so deep it can't reach the surface
And besides the skin surface is only the superficial show
And that just makes me suspicious
Deep down is the lake in Glendalough
And besides it's more important to know it
And fuck the public displays I've never trusted them
And I knew it No need to ask
But I remember you spent the first year or two singing that song to me
You And Chumbawamba
You even went down Grafton Street And bought it
And played it And sang it
I get knocked down but I get up again
I knew you meant it
I never asked
But I knew it went deeper with you by the way you used to sing that song
But I never asked you too much about before the 5th of September 1997
Because as far as I was concerned
All's that mattered was from the 5th of September 1997
But I knew by the way you used to sing that song
It went deeper
No need to ask
I knew
If you want to tell me I listen but I don't ask
But I'm sort of curious now
Or as you used to say to me
"Curious as a snake"

Chumbawamba
Now I understand for sure why you sang it
I get knocked down but I get up again
Singing And Dancing
I loved your inspirations of madness Daniela
Fitted in perfectly with mine
I loved your sappy tenderness I loved your pazz'angerness
Worse than me Worse than me
And we walked down the four flights of stairs
I knew there was a woman would climb up them four flights of stairs
with me again
"Mad Mary" was at the front hall door giving out to the traffic as usual
And I showed you the bell to ring for me
And we walked up towards "The Green"
Down Grafton Street onto Westmoreland Street
We were talking And laughing all the way down
Can't remember exactly about what
Maybe more cautiously
Had to be about the previous day
But we were getting on fine
Over the bridge onto Abbey Street
And you got your bus home to Sutton there
You gave me your phone number where you worked in the chipper
in Howth
Just for the purpose of the Shane McGowan gig
Nobody had phones in the good old days
And we kissed at your bus-stop on Abbey Street
Nobody knows me on that street
And I said I'd be back in Dublin around Tuesday or Wednesday
Probably need about at least five days to recover after that
Usually I'd have to spend at least five days recovering
Lying low under me blankets trying to remember what I'd done
And who I'd insulted
And I said I'd ring you about Shane McGowan

And I walked down to Busárus or Connolly
Can't remember which
Probably Connolly for the train
Because you could smoke And drink And piss on the train
In the good old days
And went down to Strokestown for the Agricultural Show
The annual at least five days piss-up of a bender
But you know Daniela
I came back from Strokestown the next day
Sunday
Never did that before because it was always
The annual at least five days piss-up of a bender
And I got back to the Swan that Sunday night
I think I was well on I know I was
And I rang you where you worked in the chipper in Howth
From the public telephone in the Swan
But yea if you could get me that second ticket for Shane McGowan
I'd be interested in going I'll fix you up
And I'm at home tomorrow if you're not working
Which you weren't
And you were telling me afterwards
That one of the waitresses was slagging you after I rang you chanting
"Daniela's got a boyfriend Daniela's got a boyfriend"
You loved telling me that story
Worse than me for repeating yourself
At least I'd usually have the…………
And I was telling you I should be up by 1 o' clock the next day
So if you feel like dropping over I'll be in
It's up to yourself Only if you feel like it
And I think I got up around 10 the next morning
And I'd still two or three cans in the fridge
And I was guzzling them down into me
Just to settle me down a bit
And get meself interesting

And me bell rang at 25 minutes to 1pm on the 8th of September 1997
And I'd said 1pm
And a bit of a panic
And who the fuck is this ringing me bell Upsetting me system
So I went to roll up the window
And I looked out me window from the fourth floor And you were
Down on the street at the front hall-door
Looking up at me waving And smiling
Because that first Sunday night when I slept I'd woken thinking
Last night I dreamt that somebody loved me
And you came up the four flights of stairs into my life
A life I was all prepared And set for
But a life that knew little about life
And you came into this
I was sitting on me armchair
I'd already drank me last two or three cans that were in the fridge
And you brought me two cans of Heineken And a can of Becks
And a coffee cake you'd bought in Superquinn in Sutton.

12-February-2010 York Street

Poem 54 – 26 APRILE – LIBERATION DAY – ARLUNO ONLY

I had said I wasn't going to write no more poems like this
But it's the 26th of April
Liberation Day-Arluno only
Because everywhere else in Italy it's the 25th of April
Except Arluno where the main street is named the 26th of April
But I got you the flowers yesterday
Like I do every year
And just as usual we celebrated the 25th of April
Because I always got you red carnations- i garofani rossi
On the 25th of April that would last 'til Mayday
And I told you every year when I brought them home to you
"These are for political reasons not romantic ones"
I'd always make my political non-romantic speech
And up the Partisans
A bunch of flowers for political reasons
And not a bunch of flowers for leg-opener reasons
And you agreed with me or if you didn't you didn't disagree
And get the vase And water yourself
And put them on the table
Because the 25th of April was the only time I ever got you flowers
Except for that time you had the hysterectomy in The Coombe
I brought you flowers to The Coombe maternity hospital
When they took your womb out eight years ago
You were all happy when I brought you the flowers into The Coombe
But you were also out of your head on the morphine at the time
(You told me the nurse told you the first word you said when you
woke up after the operation was "Seán" you fuckin sap)
(And just this February 2011 I found one flower
Pressed into your smemoranda diary on the page for
The 19th of October 2002 the day after your operation
I know that's one of the flowers I brought you that day Daniela
But I never knew you would of kept that you fuckin super-sap)

You'd such a bad run of luck with your health
But you never complained
You never showed it because If
You got knocked down
You got up again
If that was me I think I'd of given up a long time ago
And walked away in silence
And I still got you red carnations- i garofini rossi yesterday
For the 25th of April
Still got them still for political reasons
"Up the Partisans" "Forza Gramsci"
"Forza Fausto Bertinotti"
Questa mattina mi son svegliato bella ciao bella ciao bella ciao ciao ciao
As usual
And got the vase And the water meself
And put them on the table for you
Same spot as where you put them last year
And I had said I wasn't going to write no more poems like this
But I was thinking today
Ola this boy is crackin up this boy has broken down
That day one week after your death
And I was up at your grave in the morning
And I went back to your gaff in Via Mazzini afterwards
I was there for 11.30am
And I said to meself I'll stay there 'til 12noon
I didn't even open the shutters
Just sat there in me Italian armchair smoking And thinking
With the light on in the silence
Exactly a week after you had passed away
And I just sat there for half an hour
Thinking about 'This time last week' when you had passed away
And at 12noon I knew you had passed away
And I got that bell you had so as you could ring it
Just in case I was in the other room you could ring it

And I'd know you needed me
Just in case because sometimes your voice was too weak to call
And I got the bell at 12noon
And I rattled it
And asked you that if you could No pressure
Only if you could to give me a sign that you were alright
To let me know
And I went into the bathroom then before going out
And as I was coming out of the bathroom
I heard this music coming from your bedroom
As I was coming out of the bathroom
Rattling like a bell
And I opened the door of your bedroom
And your bedside radio had turned itself on
While I was in the bathroom Radio Popolare
But the radio stations were all static And scrambled
So I just heard "It's alright it's alright"
But the radio station was scrambling
And I was shaking the radio
But I couldn't get the station properly
Because I kept getting three or four stations mixed in together
And I could just remember "It's alright it's alright"
And I knew it was a soul motown band by the way they were singing
So I googled "It's alright it's alright soul music"
And up came The Impressions
So I youtubed it
And up came The Impressions with Curtis Mayfield
And I watched it And watched it on youtube
And I listened to the two versions on youtube
1963
I think you liked Curtis Mayfield
But I can't really recall you mentioning him
But there's two videos of it
Where The Impressions are singing *Its Alright It's Alright*

And one of them has women dancing in it
The exact same way you used to dance
Because that's a song you could dance to
So maybe it was an electrical fault
Or maybe I'm not so technological
And I can't even turn off a radio properly
But it never happened before
And I know it was you that turned on your bedside radio
And you said "It's alright It's alright"
And I had said I wasn't going to write no more poems like this
But then what about that snail
The day after I threw the two snails from your grave
And I went to sit on the balcony at about 7am the next morning
Drinking me coffee smoking And thinking
And where I sit
What's sitting on the balcony railing right in front of me
Right in front of where I sat in the mornings on top of the balcony railing
Right in front of my nose at eye level
Only a snail
Just one snail
Out of her shell looking at me
And I don't know much about snails
But I know that snail was female
So I sat looking at her
Drinking me coffee smoking And thinking
And wondering how she got there
Hadn't rained the night before Ground was dry
So it would be impossible for a snail to get there
Unless that snail was a certain female I once knew
And I took that female snail after
And I hid her in Nina's flower-box
Before Nina saw her And wanted to throw her again
I looked in the flower-box the next day but she was gone
I was planning on keeping her as a pet but she was gone

Coincidence or me gone into a shell
Or just signs of comfort from you
But it's easier for me now to believe in that now
Than for me to believe in a miracle
Yea I'm the fuckin eejit who believed in a miracle
And that's not because I'm naïve because I'm not because
I had said I wasn't going to write no more poems like this
But I still go into Whitefriar Street Church
Just every Friday now
And I don't bother with San Antonio
I keep to the other side of the church now because
I was with San Antonio over the other side of the church for
eighteen months
No hard feelings
So I just don't bother with him anymore
Because every Friday now I keep to the other side
And I go to San Valentino
I know he's an Italian as well
Probably all great mates together with
San Antonio San Pellegrino San Francesco San Pio
Probably all great mates with them having a good laugh together
None of them done nothing for you
Probably all too busy laughing And saying "Mamma Mia" to each other
And slapping their hands off their knees
So I don't say nothing to San Valentino
Don't even look at him
I just light my candle
And I say my prayer to your face in the candle's smiling flame
Just a quick prayer in hope to the flame that
There is a light that never goes out And
I WILL SEE YOUR FACE AGAIN
And I walk back out down the church again
And I don't even look over towards San Antonio
Because San Antonio can go And fuck off with himself now because

"Nobody kicks me up the arse woman or man or saint And gets away
with it"
Because I'm with The Impressions now
Or Curtis Mayfield And his new band "The Snails"
And they're saying *"It's All Right It's All Right"*
And I know you are
So I'm saying
I'm not going to write no more poems like this.

26-April-2010 York Street

Poem 55 – MAY BANK HOLIDAY SUNDAY MORNING
– *ON THE BEACH*

The world is turning I hope it don't turn away
I was in "The Green" there just over an hour ago Daniela
Early About 9.30am Nobody there
I had some bread-rolls left over so I said to meself
I'd bring them into "The Green" to distribute a bit of breakfast
There'd never be any bread left over if you were here
Because you loved your bread
Just like Pasquale
And I had some bread-rolls left over so I said to meself
I'd bring them into "The Green" to distribute a bit of breakfast
Because it was early About 9.30am Nobody there
I used to go in there every Sunday morning
When we first moved back to York Street last year
Always sat on the same spot on the same bench
I used to think about things
This morning I remembered what I used to think about but more so
I remembered what I used not to think
I finally acknowledged it
"I fuckin knew alright"
Because I used to think you wouldn't be here much longer
And when I'd get home you wouldn't be here much longer
I thought of that this morning
And I brought over the bread-rolls with me
I was looking for the seagulls
Because a seagull shat on the glass of the balcony last November
And it wasn't one of those dainty cute cuddly little bits of shit either
But a big post-modernist arty splatter of a one
And it took me ages to scrub it off
So I went looking for the seagulls in "The Green"
Because now I'm living out here on the beach
But those seagulls are still out of reach
But those seagulls I couldn't see any of them

Only ducks One swan One pigeon came along after
And I don't know why people don't like seagulls
And first to come along was one duck
And I threw him some bread
Then all his mates started arriving
And I threw them some bread
And then one swan came along
And I threw him some bread
But if there had of been two swans together I'd resolved that
They would of got nothing from me
I'd already decided that beforehand
But it was just one swan on his own
So I threw him some bread
And then a pigeon came along later
And I threw him some bread
And when the bread was gone I went
And sat on the same spot on the same bench
And I thought what I used to think
And I thought more so what I used not to think
There was nobody there
A shower of rain had come down just beforehand
Because I need a crowd of people but I can't face them day to day
Sunday mornings there last year
Then I'd come back home to you after
And you were still here
And I sat on the bench smoking And thinking
And thinking about the seagulls
That even if one of them did shit all over the glass on the balcony
That in future I will just give bread to the seagulls
I will just feed the seagulls
Because I like the seagulls
Because nobody else does
Because the world is turning I just don't want to see it turn away.

2-May-2010 York Street

Poem 56 – ROCK AND ROLL

I was standing inside the glass door of McCann's Hardware
At Leonard's Corner there this morning
Watching out into the yard
Watching out into the rain pissing down
Craning me neck to scrutinise the clouds
Wondering how much longer it could go on for
The sky was blue though *Ma il cielo è sempre più blu*
Up around Kilmainham direction
And then the rain seemed to ease
But it was only taking a breather
For it down poured again
And I was wondering how much longer it could go on for
How much more it had left
It can't keep raining
It has to stop sometime
And I wanted to witness the last droplet of rain that fell
Wanted to watch it falling
To identify it
And catch it in my palm
Before it hit the ground I'd be out through that glass door
And catch it in my palm And say to it
"Congratulations You are the last drop of rain"
But then the rain seemed to ease And I couldn't wait any longer
I had a few things to do
And besides nobody has ever seen the last droplet of rain falling
So I walked out into the ceasing rain
I think that last droplet of rain fell sometime somewhere
As I was walking down the South Circular Road towards Kelly's Corner
It just stopped as the sky cleared from
Up around Kilmainham direction
But nobody spoke of it
I would of liked to have waited for that last droplet of rain

To know what it looked And felt like
To know it had stopped
To know it was over
But I had a few things to do
And on Wexford Street I went into the greengrocers
They had the radio on
And I bought one carrot And four mushrooms Forty-two cents
And Robert Plant came on the radio
And he was singing about how
It's been a long time been a long time been a long time been a long
lonely lonely lonely lonely lonely time
I knew what he meant
If it had still been raining
I could of stalled inside the greengrocers door
And listened to the end of the song
But it had stopped raining
So I'd no excuse to stall I had to move on
And walk out into the world again
And come home to the gaff here
And get used to not coming home to you But
I won't leave you.

Seán Caomhánach 22-September-2010 Sráid Eabhrac Baile Átha Cliath
Ireland 32

EPILOGUE

AMARCORD

It must of been about five or six years ago
And I was sitting on me armchair
And you were sitting on your couch
And we were watching that episode of The Simpsons on the telly
one evening
And it was that episode
Where Bart had done some destruction in the school
And the teachers in a protest went out on strike
Or something like that
So that the parents of the students had to come into the school
In the evening instead as substitutes for the teachers
And teach the students
Or something like that
And Homer got the job of teaching an evening in Bart's school
But the first class he taught in it
Nobody was interested in what he was saying
And Homer was upset about this
That nobody was interested in what he was saying
So for his next lesson
He started talking about more personal things
And he started talking about
The domestic And intimate details of his marriage to Marge
And these details got a great reception
And everyone was interested in what he was saying
And even Barney And Moe
And all his mates from the bar And work
Were in the classroom
To hear what he was saying about
The domestic And intimate details of his marriage to Marge
But Marge wasn't too impressed

When she learnt the reason as to why
Homer's school-teaching was so popular
And packing them into the school every evening
But Homer was delighted with himself
That his school-teaching was so popular
And that the students were interested in what he was saying
And he didn't really cop the real reason for this
And I was sitting on me armchair
And you were sitting on your couch
And we were both laughing our heads off
Watching that episode of The Simpsons
And when it was over
I leaned over towards you
And I said
"That's like the sort of thing that I'd do"
And you said
"I know"
And we were both laughing our heads off
Because that's exactly what I've done
But how did you know Daniela
There is no end to this
I have seen your face.

29-January-2011 York Street

SONG TITLES AND LYRICS IN 30 POEMS TO DANIELA

1. *Waiting For The Sun* – The Doors (Song Title)
2. *On The Beach* – Neil Young (Song Title – Poem1)
3. *Ambulance Blues* – Neil Young (Song Title – Poem 1)
4. *Don't walk away in silence* – Joy Division (**Song Lyrics from "Atmosphere"** – Poem 2)
5. *Into My Arms* – Nick Cave (Song Title)
6. *A Pair Of Brown Eyes* – The Pogues (Song Title – Poem 4)
7. *And I'm not happy and I'm not sad* – The Smiths (**Song Lyrics from "This Night Has Opened My Eyes"** – Poem 8)
8. *Ain't nobody that can sing like me*- Billy Bragg (**Song Lyrics Written By Woodie Guthrie From "Way Over Yonder In The Minor Key"** – Poems 13,53)
9. *Walking the streets in the rain* – Butch Moore (**Song Title from "Walking The Streets In The Rain"** – Poem 19)
10. *Hi hello wake from thy sleep God has given your soul to keep all of the power that burns in the flame Ignites the light in a single name.* – Patti Smith (**Song lyrics from "Frederick"** – Poem 22)
11. *Sultans Of Swing* – Dire Straits (Song Title – Poem 22)
12. *The measure of my dreams* – The Pogues (**Song Lyrics from "Rainy Night In Soho"** – Poem 24)
13. *We Don't Need Nobody Else* – Whipping Boy (Song Title – Poem 27)
14. *In the middle of the night I call your name* – John Lennon (**Song Lyrics from "Oh Yoko"** – Poem 28)
15. *When I'm 64*-The Beatles (Song Title – Poem 28)
16. *Ain't No Sunshine* – Bill Withers (Song Title – Poem 30)
17. *Riders On The Storm* – The Doors (Song Title – Poem 33)
18. *Girl you gotta love your man Girl you gotta love your man Take him by the hand Make him understand The world on us depends our lives can never end Yeah* – The Doors (**Song Lyrics from "Riders on The Storm"** – Poem 33)
19. *The Weeping Song* – Nick Cave (Song Title – Poem 34)

20. *This is the weeping song* – Nick Cave (**Song Lyrics from "The Weeping Song"** – Poem 34)

21. *Good times for a change please please please let me let me* – The Smiths (**Song Lyrics from "Please Please Please Let Me Get What I Want"** – Poem 36)

22. *Good times for a change you see the luck that I've had can make a good man turn bad* – The Smiths (Song Lyrics – Poem 36)

23. *Because the life that I've had can make a good man bad* – The Smiths (Song Lyrics – Poem 36)

24. *In this place filled with empty space Your love holds the key baby sympathise with me I need you before I lost your touch of life and grace I knew that your sweet face could always comfort me* – Robin Trower (**Song Lyrics from "In This Place"** – Poem 38)

25. *Yesterday* – The Beatles (Song Title – Poem 39)

26. *Scooping the bowl of beans spreading them like stars* – Thin Lizzy (**Song Lyrics from "The Friendly Ranger at Clontarf Castle"** – Poem 39)

27. *I Wanna Be Sedated* – The Ramones (Song Title – Poem 41)

28. *I wanna live* – The Ramones (Song Title – Poem 41)

29. *When The Music's Over* – The Doors (Song Title – Poem 43)

30. *And if I don't meet you no more in this world I'll meet you in the next one don't be late don't be late* – Jimi Hendrix (**Song Lyrics from "Voodoo Chile"** – Poems 43,48)

31. *Bad Moon Rising* – Creedence Clearwater Revival (Song Title – Poem 43)

32. *Thank You For The Day* – Kirsty McColl (Song Title written by Ray Davies – The Kinks – Poem 44)

33. *The Only Mistake* – Joy Division (Song Title – Poem 45)

34. *Dead Can Dance* – The Name Of A Band – Poem 47

35. *Foxy Lady* – Jimi Hendrix (Song Title – Poem 47)

36. *The KKK Took My Baby Away* – The Ramones (Song Title – Poem 48)

37. *Niente Paura* – Ligabue (Song Title – Poems 48, 53)

38. *Wake up you sleepy head* – David Bowie (**Song Lyrics from "Oh You Pretty Things"** – Poem 48)

39. *Wake up and make love with me Wake up and make love*- Ian Dury And The Blockheads (**Song Lyrics from "Wake Up and Make Love With Me"** – Poem 48

40. *There Is A Light That Never Goes Out* – The Smiths (Song Title – Poem 53)

41. *Take me out tonight Because I want to see people And I want to see life*- The Smiths (**Song Lyric from "There Is A light That Never Goes Out"** – Poem 53)

42. *First rule is* – The Ramones (**Song Lyric from "Commando"** – Poem 53)

43. *And if a double-decker bus Crashes into us To die by your side Is such a heavenly way to die* – The Smiths (**Song Lyrics from "There Is A Light That Never Goes Out"** – Poem 53)

44. *Oh what difference does it make None at all* – The Smiths (**Song lyrics from "Oh What Difference Does It Make"** – Poem 53)

45. *What have I become My sweetest friend* – Johnny Cash/ Nine Inch Nails (**Song Lyrics from "Hurt"** – Poem 53)

46. *I hurt myself today To see if I still feel I focus on the pain The only thing that's real* – Johnny Cash/ Nine Inch Nails (**Song Lyrics from "Hurt"** – Poem 53)

47. *I'm deep inside myself but I'll get out somehow* – Neil Young (**Song Lyrics from "Motion Pictures"** – Poem 53)

48. *Last Night I Dreamt That Somebody Loved Me* – The Smiths (Song Title – Poem 53)

49. *And if a ten-ton truck Kills the both of us To die by your side The pleasure the privilege is mine* – The Smiths (**Song Lyrics from "There Is A Light That Never Goes Out"** – Poem 53)

50. *Hello I love you won't you tell me your name* – The Doors (**Song Lyrics from "Hello I Love You"** – Poem 53)

51. *I'm a million miles away I'm a million miles away Sailing like a driftwood on a windy day* – Rory Gallagher (**Song Lyrics from "A Million Miles Away"** – Poem 53)

52. *I'm a lucky man* – The Verve
(**Song Lyrics from "Lucky Man"** – Poem 53)

53. *I get knocked down but I get up again* – Chumbawamba (Song Title – Poem 53)

54. *I had said I wasn't going to write no more poems like this* – Gil Scott-Heron (**Song Lyrics from "Jose Campos Torres"** – Poem 54)

55. *Questa mattina mi son svegliato bella ciao bella ciao bella ciao ciao ciao* – Modena City Ramblers – (Song Lyrics but a traditional ballad – Poem 54)

56. *This boy is cracking up This boy has broken down* – Phil Lynott (**Song Lyrics from "Old Town"** – Poem 54)

57. *It's Alright It's Alright* – The Impressions (Song Title – Poem 54)

58. *The world is turning I hope it don't turn away* – Neil Young (**Song Lyrics from "On The Beach"** – Poem 55)

59. *Because now I'm living out here on the beach but those seagulls are still out of reach* – Neil Young (**Song Lyrics from "On The Beach"** – Poem 55)

60. *Because I need a crowd of people but I can't face them day to day* – Neil Young (**Song Lyrics from "On The Beach"** – Poem 55)

61. *Because the world is turning I just don't want to see it turn away* – Neil Young (**Song Lyrics from "On The Beach"** – Poem 55)

62. *Ma il cielo è sempre più blu* – Rino Gaetano (Song Title – Poem 56)

63. *It's been a long time been a long time been a long time been a long lonely lonely lonely lonely lonely lonely time* – Led Zeppelin (**Song Lyrics from "Rock And Roll"** – Poem 56)

64. *There is no end to this, I have seen your face* – New Order (**Song Lyrics from "Procession"** – Poem 56)